THE ART of WORSHIP

THE ACT of WORSHIP

THE ART of WORSHIP

A MUSICIAN'S GUIDE TO LEADING MODERN WORSHIP

GREG SCHEER

BakerBooks

a division of Baker Publishing Group
Grand Rapids, Michigan

Published by Baker Books
a division of Baker Publishing Group
P.O. Box 6287, Grand Rapids, MI 49516-6287
www.bakerbooks.com

Printed in the United States of America

Library of Congress Cataloging-in-Publication Data
Scheer, Greg, 1966–
    The art of worship : a musician's guide to leading modern worship / Greg Scheer.
        p.   cm.
    Includes bibliographical references.
    ISBN 10: 0-8010-6709-X (pbk.)
    ISBN 978-0-8010-6709-9 (pbk.)
        1. Public worship. I. Title.
BV15.S333 2006
264—dc22   2006023524

This book is dedicated to Kirstin, Christine, Tony, Anila, Angela, Andrew, Lea, Beth, Andrea, Lois, Laura, Matt, Andy, Lucas, Alaina, Rachel, Charity, Sarah, Jodi, and Erin, who helped me develop this material in the classroom. This book wouldn't be what it is without you. And to Amy: I wouldn't be who I am without you.

CONTENTS

INTRODUCTION

MY JOURNEY INTO WORSHIP
(OR, CONFESSIONS OF A FAILED ROCK STAR)

I never wanted to be a music minister.

I scoffed at those who "couldn't make it in the real world"—those who I felt were retreating from a Christian musician's true calling to be salt and light, opting instead for the safety offered inside the church walls. You have to understand that this was a time when Amy Grant was cutting-edge contemporary Christian music, and "Our God Reigns" was pushing the boundaries of modern worship. I was repulsed by the musical mediocrity that I saw in the Christian community and felt that I would make my mark like other Christians who were taking their music to the highways and byways—U2, Bruce Cockburn, T Bone Burnett.

But God had different plans.

After growing up in an independent Pentecostal church, a Bible-belt oddity in the predominantly Roman Catholic Rhode Island, I spent my college years church hopping. I attended two Baptist churches, one Episcopal, and a variety of others. By the time I was a junior, my faith was wasting away. I was more inspired by the post-punk angst I heard in my favorite bands—Joe Jackson, Talking Heads, Elvis Costello—than I was by the churches I attended.

Worship music wasn't even on my radar. In fact, the first time I led worship, I don't know if I even would have called myself a Christian. I had long, nappy hair and wore jeans, pajama tops, and black boots, which made me very desirable for a particular youth minister who thought I would make a great trophy if I converted. He roped me into playing my guitar at a weekend retreat, and any honest account would call it a disaster. The only song I remember playing was "Come, Let Us Worship and Bow Down"; how could I have known that it was a worship ballad and not a Violent Femmes acoustic thrash?

The following year I studied in Salzburg, Austria. It was a turning point in my faith journey. Ironically, the Lord used my time in a post-Christian European culture to build my waning faith from the ground up. I came to realize that I had been using minor grievances with the American Christian subculture to avoid Jesus Christ and his claim on my life. I finally gave in to "the hound of heaven." Faithful (and patient) Christian friends in Austria helped me grow in my new faith, and I returned to the United States committed to living my life for Christ.

By the time I got to grad school in Pittsburgh, I was concentrating more seriously on composing modern art music than I was on my rock and roll, but I still had no interest in using my musical skills in the church. However, I joined the choir at Bellefield Presbyterian Church, where I got my first vision for music ministry. I started to realize that worship music wasn't B-grade secular music; it was music that served a particular purpose—the praise of God. I fell in love with many other aspects of music ministry as well: the community that forms within the church music groups, the creativity and variety of worship music through the ages, and the nurturing of young believers as they interact with other Christians.

I soon began to entertain thoughts of becoming involved in music ministry. At the same time, the current music minister began to entertain thoughts of concentrating more time on his counseling practice, and I was asked to take over. It seems odd that a former church-music-hater would be employed as a church-music-maker, but it is obvious now that this is the vocation the Lord had been preparing me for. Suddenly the circuitous route that I had followed made sense, with my composition background, experience in rock and jazz, and training in conducting all having application in music ministry. God surely moves in mysterious ways. The twelve years since Bellefield have been filled with music ministry: at Wildwood Presbyterian in Florida, Northwestern College in Iowa, and now Church of the Servant Christian Reformed Church and the Calvin Institute of Christian Worship in Grand Rapids, Michigan.

About This Book

Two worlds collide in today's worship: the world of the classically trained organist, choir director, or music minister, and the world of the play-by-ear, chord-chart-reading pop musician. Although these worlds have much in common, they rarely meet and they have no common language. It is my contention that each of these musical worlds has strengths and weaknesses and much to learn from each other. Wouldn't it be wonderful if *all* musicians could read music and improvise and take part in our rich church music heritage at the same time as being energized by the new forms of popular, folk, and ethnic music that blow across our modern worship landscape?

Regardless of where you stand in the spectrum of historic and modern worship expressions, you must acknowledge the reality that many churches now employ some form of worship team (often called a praise team or praise band) in their services. If you are a "traditional" music minister, you will be involved in directing, overseeing, or collaborating with a worship team soon, if you aren't already. This book will give you the tools to interact successfully with what may be an unfamiliar genre to you. If you are a "contemporary" music minister, this book will help you think more deeply about the theology of church song, the flow of liturgy, and aspects of music you may have previously only considered intuitively.

My goal is not to convince traditional church musicians to defect into the contemporary camp. In fact, I'm not interested in entering into stylistic debate at all. I take the view that "all musics are created equal,"[1] that "'everything is permissible for me'—but not everything is beneficial" (1 Cor. 6:12), and that we all have to work through issues of worship style "with fear and trembling" (Phil. 2:12). My hope is to enable church musicians of all kinds to better understand one of the dominant musical languages of modern worship, to be thoroughly equipped to lead that style, and to foster communication among the musicians of the church of Jesus Christ.

Defining the Terms

Before venturing any further, it is important to articulate what the subject is, and what it is not.

What Is Contemporary Worship?

Contemporary. The word *contemporary* is derived from the root words *con* and *tempus*, or "with the times." Therefore, a generous definition of contemporary worship music should include Arvo Pärt's "Magnificat," modern hymns by Erik Routley, the techno-worship of Grace, and the meditative chants of Taizé. It could even include the worship music of the past that is used in living traditions—Charles Wesley, Sacred Harp, Thomas Tallis, and medieval plainchant. All of these are "with the times" in the sense that they are still in use today. However, the common understanding of the word is something that is current, up-to-date, and usually cutting edge. Thus, the Spice Girls are considered ancient history though they've been off the pop charts only a few years.

While some critics argue that contemporary worship should be defined more inclusively, in practice it has come to mean a particular style of worship practiced by a particular kind of church. When the semantic dust settles, "contemporary worship music" has come to mean a musical style that originates in contemporary popular culture rather than in church culture.

Worship. John Witvliet has observed that there are three overlapping definitions of worship.[2] The broadest definition is "worship in all of life." As Romans 12:1 tells us, true worship is offering our lives to God. The second definition is the "worship service," the time in which the body of Christ gathers to perform specific acts of worship. The most recent and narrow definition of the word *worship* is the "music portion of the worship service," as in, "The praise team will now lead us in worship."

Before discussing worship, we must clarify which definition is being used: faithful mopping of floors is one way a janitor worships God, but it is not part of a worship service; music is an important part of the worship service, but it certainly shouldn't displace other acts of worship such as Holy Communion or reading Scripture.

Though I encourage a broad view of worship, in this book we'll restrict our discussions primarily to the musical forms of worship used in church services. Further, while I embrace an approach to musical style that is "deep and wide," in this book the focus is music of the Praise & Worship genre. Finally, words such as *contemporary, traditional, modern, praise band,* and *worship team* may have different connotations for different readers. I will try to be as precise as possible in the way I use these words and pray that the terms I use won't confuse the meaning of the text.

What Is "Praise & Worship"?

A misnomer. The phrase "Praise & Worship" comes from the idea that praise, or talking *about* God, leads to worship, talking *to* God. In fact, *worship* is an umbrella term that incorporates praise, lament, confession, and many other acts of worship. To join these two terms makes no more sense than joining "lament and worship" or "armadillos and animals." However, I've become tired of fingering quotation marks in the air every time I speak the phrase "Praise & Worship," so I've given in. Praise & Worship is the most common term for the genre, and it will be used here.

A tradition. For all the talk of freedom of worship and relevance to the culture, Praise & Worship has itself become a tradition. It has roots in the Jesus movement of the 60s, black gospel, Pentecostalism, and popular music styles. In its thirty-year history, it has become the dominant music style of the evangelical church. In fact, further evidence that Praise & Worship is a tradition is that there are now alternative worship movements breaking away from it.

A style. Theoretically, Praise & Worship could take any culturally relevant musical form, but in practice it is marked by a fairly distinct style. The lyrics are uplifting, the beat is modern but tame, and the vocals feature rich harmonies. Essentially, it is easy-listening music played by a pop band in a church.

An industry. Behind the Praise & Worship songs that are sung in local churches each Sunday is a multimillion-dollar worship industry. Music businesses that began by selling albums from the backs of vans in church parking lots have grown into hugely profitable companies that sell worship "products" ranging from CDs to worship aerobic videos. Even secular companies want a piece of the action: Chevy was the corporate sponsor of the "Come Together and Worship" tour, and a number of secular companies have forged distribution deals or outright purchases of Praise & Worship publishers. Whether the industry has sold its soul to the devil or not is hard to say, but profit is certainly one of its major motivations.

Why Is Praise & Worship Important?

A quickly growing worship style. Like it or not, Praise & Worship is a significant—if not the most significant—force in today's worship. Though countercultural when the movement began, today it is thoroughly mainstream, with even the most traditional churches including songs such as "As the Deer" and "In Christ Alone" in their worship. Many new churches—most notably the seeker movement—are founded on the musical style, while older churches are starting new services to meet the demand for Praise & Worship.

A common musical language. Pop music is the *lingua franca* of today's musical world. Drums and electric guitars, which once outraged older generations, now appear in everything from television advertisements to shopping-mall soundtracks. Like all pop music, the light rock sound of Praise & Worship is a common denominator among the people in the pews.

An inevitability. Worship music has always been a merger of the church's tradition and vernacular influences. It seems inevitable that

Praise & Worship will eventually graft itself into the church's tradition in the same way that medieval German *leisen*, gospel songs, and folk traditions have become a part of today's tradition.

How Has Praise & Worship Changed Worship?

Shift of spiritual perspective. Not only did the Jesus movement produce a change in music style, it also precipitated a shift to a more intimate way of worshiping. The previous generation had viewed worship primarily as a learning experience: hymns were pedagogical tools, liturgy was crafted around a theme, and sermons led to a more enlightened view of the Christian experience. But today's worshipers long for worship that engages them emotionally. No longer is Jesus a distant God whom one goes to church to learn *about*; he is a personal God whom one goes to church to talk *to*.

Expanded worship expressions. The Pentecostal roots of Praise & Worship have led to an increased use of biblical worship expressions. Thirty years ago, a worshiper with hands raised in praise may have been escorted from the church, but today hand-raising is common even in mainline denominations. Worship is no longer an exercise of the mind; it is an expression of the body and emotions as well.

New musical paradigm. For centuries, church music has been some combination of voice and keyboard with a sprinkling of other instruments. In some generations a cappella singing reigned; in others the organ or piano led. Epochs of richer instrumentation have come and gone; different approaches to text and music have flourished and faded. But today, rhythm rules. Rock-and-roll dance rhythms led by a band have replaced vocally driven worship forms led by choir, organ, or congregation.

Change in leadership. Worship used to be led by the pastor and organist. The pastor determined liturgy and perhaps chose congregational hymns. The organist was the primary worship leader, leading the congregation's singing and providing musical selections such as the prelude and offertory. Today, worship leaders often shape all but the sermon. At their worst they are minor celebrities who hijack the worship experience with manipulative show-business techniques, but at their best they are leaders who model authentic worship and choose music that empowers the people to express themselves to God.

Increased awareness. One of the positive results of the worship upheavals over the last thirty years is an increased awareness of the importance of worship. People today may differ about worship, but at least they care. This was not the case a short time ago, when many considered everything else in the service a warm-up to the sermon. Today there is increased dialogue about worship, and Christians are more passionate and engaged in the total worship experience, regardless of the style.

1

SETTING THE STAGE

Afew years ago, I was asked to help the worship committee of a large, established church in a rural setting that was considering the addition of a contemporary worship service. As I talked with the committee members, it became apparent that they didn't want advice; they wanted a blessing. An additional music ensemble would stretch their already meager pool of musicians. A new service would take a substantial financial commitment—one they were clearly not willing to make. If their goal was to reach out to the lost, I asked them, wouldn't it make more sense to add a Spanish service for the new Latino immigrants in their area rather than add another service option for their town's over-churched longtime residents?

All my questions fell on deaf ears. The worship committee members were convinced that a contemporary service would revitalize their church; the infighting and lack of spiritual fervor that had marked their congregation for the last fifty years would be healed with a new style of music. I left the meeting saddened that they were unwilling to be honest with themselves.

A few months later, a volunteer musician from the church called me. Evidently she didn't know about my earlier consultation with the worship committee, because she explained that they were starting a new service and that they needed musicians. I asked what she needed to fill out her ensembles, and she answered, "Piano, bass, guitar, drums, maybe some singers." "When does the new service begin?" I asked. "In a little under a month," was the answer. "You mean to tell me that you're starting a new service in a few weeks and you don't have a team together?" I asked incredulously.

I visited the service a few months later, and my fears were confirmed. The "contemporary" music was hardly contemporary and certainly not anything that would draw people on its own merit. The musical and logistical preparation was half-baked. And the skit that was meant to bring home the point of the service was something that must have tried the patience of even the parents of the high school actors who performed it.

Repeat after me:

Contemporary worship music will not revitalize my church.
Contemporary worship music will not revitalize my church.
Contemporary worship music will not revitalize my church.

Unfortunately, this story is repeated over and over again in churches that are unwilling to honestly assess their worship situation and unwilling to adequately prepare for a new service or style of music.

Assess Your Church's Situation

If you work in a church, you know that music is the flash point for many conflicts. If a musical change is not itself the source of tension, it is the battlefield upon which other conflicts are played out. But music can also be a source of great unity. Worship wars can often be avoided by taking honest inventory of a church's situation before making any changes in music style.

Assess the Congregation

Do the people need new music? Of course; every congregation needs to regularly freshen their worship with new songs. But does your congregation need a significantly different repertoire than it currently uses? Perhaps a better way to ask this question is: "Do the people sing enthusiastically?" If your church has a vibrant worship life with its current music, leave it alone!

I heard of one church that had a long history of excellent choirs, fine organists, and vibrant congregational singing. A new pastor came in, convinced that contemporary worship music was what the church needed, and he proceeded to clean house. A choir program that had included over two hundred members from children to seniors was replaced by praise teams, and organists were replaced by guitarists; needless to say, the director who had worked so hard to build the music ministry was no longer welcome. In a few months, the pastor destroyed something that had taken years to build and replaced it with distrust and disunity. He failed to recognize that every congregation is unique and that its worship should have a unique worship personality.

Who makes up this congregation, and are they being represented musically? Sometimes a church changes musical styles because some people in the church are being left out musically. For instance, there may be growing youth attendance but no change in the worship service that reflects this changing demographic. Perhaps a minority group could be explicitly welcomed by the inclusion of music from their worship traditions. This is not to say that a church should slavishly represent the demographics of its people, but it should give every person a sense of ownership and belonging.

Does the proposed change come from the people? If a musical change is one person's pet project, it is bound to fail. If it was initiated by the congregation on a grassroots level, it will enjoy broad support when officially introduced. For example, one church in which I served had little problem introducing new music into Sunday morning worship. How did this church avoid conflict? They had a college fellowship that sang Praise & Worship, a Sunday evening "prayer and praise" service, and numerous retreats that used modern worship music. By the time we regularly began including a worship team in the Sunday morning worship, most of the congregation had already sung Praise & Worship in a positive setting.

Are there special considerations that must be made when introducing a new music style into a particular congregation? Every church has their quirks and history, and these must be taken into account. Perhaps the church is a historic building with a beautiful altar area; this is not the place to propose the installation of a projection screen. Perhaps there is a faction in the church that feels drums have no place in a church sanctuary; introduce new music with just piano and guitar, or ask the group how they would feel about hand percussion. If the church has a history of excellent choirs, make the choir director an ally rather than an enemy.

The goal is not to have cutting-edge worship; it is to have engaging worship that gives the people a voice in their praise of God.

Assess Resources

If you don't have enough musicians or sufficient financial resources to support a new worship style, it won't matter if your congregation is ready for change. Before proposing any changes to the church's leadership, you must count the cost.

Who will lead the new worship team (or teams)? Every ensemble needs a skilled leader. Any proposal for a new worship style needs to include a recommendation for a worship team leader who is trusted by the music minister, the church, and the musicians. Is it you? You may know about aspects of modern worship leadership, but perhaps you think that you don't have enough experience or that Praise & Worship is just not "your thing." Is there someone in your congregation who is more suited to leading the new team? If so, is the person willing to volunteer, or will he or she be paid (and how much)? Is it a person who will build consensus or cause division over the new music style? Is he or she truly skilled, or just available?

If there is no suitable leader from within the congregation, do you want to hire someone from the outside? A "hired gun" may do a skilled job of leading, but he or she will cost the church significantly more money and will probably not be as emotionally invested in the ministry as an insider would be. Also, if you have to look outside the church for a team leader, that may be an indication that the time is not right for a new worship team. A church's worship should grow from the people; if no one from the church can lead a particular style of music, perhaps God is calling you to wait. This is not a hard and fast rule. Oftentimes all the elements of a ministry are assembled except one; in such a case, hiring one person will mobilize the whole ministry.

Who are the key musicians? While advising one church about their plans to start a contemporary worship service, I asked which musicians were available for such a venture. They admitted that they didn't have many good candidates; they had a few high school kids but no seasoned musicians who would be willing to commit to the team before plans started. This is extremely dangerous. Every team needs "backbone musicians" who can be counted on for their musicianship and commitment. Auditions will flesh out the team, but start your plans for a new team with some idea of who will play the piano or guitar.

What physical resources are available? Music-making costs money. Does your church have the equipment needed to successfully start a new worship team? Major investments may include an adequate sound system and possibly a projection screen, both of which can cost thousands of dollars. Most churches need to buy their own drum set and keyboard. Additionally, you must budget for ongoing music purchases, supplies, and appropriate licenses.

How much money is needed to launch the worship team? Church leaders will be concerned about the bottom line, as they should be. Your proposal should detail the cost of outfitting a new worship team. Handing the church elders a proposal that will cost the church twenty thousand dollars may be frightening, but it is better for them to know the cost up front rather than surprising them later.

It is important that you receive the church's financial support for a new worship team. Jesus says that where your treasure is, there your heart will be also. Church leaders who approve a new worship team but don't approve the money to support it are communicating that they don't value it as much as other initiatives that they do fund. Apathy or resistance in the beginning stages of worship change indicates that there will not be broad support for the change from the congregation. It also means that the new worship team will be at a disadvantage as they try to introduce the new music.

Assess the Leadership

Church politics are a tricky business. In the worst cases, there are angry divisions between different groups in the church, competing visions between the pastor and congregation, or small factions that are willing to destroy the church to make a point about long-standing feuds. Even in healthy churches, there are many sides to every story and many needs that must be balanced in every decision. We must respect these authorities that God has set up in our churches, and we must be wise in the way we present music initiatives to them—as wise as serpents and as harmless as doves.

What is the pastor's vision? If the pastor doesn't support a change in worship, it will fail. The work and vision of the music minister must complement the pastor's. Certainly you should make your opinions known to the pastor, but ultimately the vision that is cast to the elders and congregation must come from the pastor. Once the vision is caught and the proposed worship change is accepted, your work will be to implement the change.

You must also ascertain the pastor's ability to carry out the vision. I once was a worship consultant in a church whose pastor valued consensus above all things. In this particular church, consensus was almost impossible. On the one hand, the associate pastor had a vision for contemporary worship that he thought would revitalize the aging congregation, a vision he was aggressively spreading throughout the youth, singles, and church staff. On the other hand, the music minister was a classically trained musician who had been hired to carry on the choral tradition for which the church was known. The pastor was unable or unwilling to cast a unified vision for the church's worship, so the conflict between the associate pastor and music minister, and their respective followers, raged on. In fact, ten years later the conflict still rages on, though both the associate pastor and music minister have been replaced. The lesson is clear: don't rally for a change that the pastor doesn't support enough to see through to completion.

Is there support from the elders? The elders give an accurate picture of how the whole congregation will react to a change in worship. Listen to their counsel. If they affirm using modern music within worship but are against creating a new service, submit to their decision. If they have reservations about an aspect of your proposal, address the issue with them; otherwise you will be forced to address it again with the whole congregation. If you can get the elders excited about a worship change, each one of them will spread the vision to their spouses, friends, and small groups. Therefore, it is important that you have a collaborative relationship with them.

Will a change in music style promote a particular group? In my experience, the push for a new type of music in worship usually comes from a vocal minority who have experienced it and find it meaningful: youth, charismatics, or a particular "cell" group. It is great that these groups are passionate about worship and it is good to capitalize on their energy, but take care that it doesn't seem you are promoting a particular group or demographic at the expense of others. Let's say the youth come back from a retreat fired up about worship. They ask if some new songs can be included in worship and even form a band to lead the songs. The larger congregation may view this as a "kid thing." They may even be wondering why the youth get to add their favorite music to the services, while the older members' request for a hymn sing was never granted. All in all it's healthier to choose music that may highlight a particular group but benefits the whole congregation.

What is the church's worship history? I once worked in a church that had an ongoing rift between longtime members who were loyal to the denomination and more evangelically minded members from the nearby university. Sometimes this rift played itself out in battles over new worship styles, going back as far as the Jesus movement of the 60s. In situations like this, churches must take great care not to open old wounds. Instead, they should move ahead slowly, presenting new initiatives in a way that avoids the "us and them" mentality of previous worship changes.

Assess Your Own Motives

Assessing your church's pastor, elders, and congregation without searching your own heart would be disingenuous. Why do you want to introduce a change to your church's worship? Do you truly believe that a new style of music will revitalize your church's worship, or are you just trying to "keep up with the Joneses"? There are simply too many churches that jump into worship changes, producing more harm than good. True, many worship wars are due to hard hearts, but sometimes conflicts are created by leaders with agendas that don't ultimately serve the people. A new music style may be just what is needed in your church, but you must be willing to let it go if it's not right for your church.

Spread the Vision

Charles Arn argues that any initiative requiring change in a church will be met by five response groups: Innovators (2 percent), who dream up ideas for change; Early Adopters (18 percent), who know a good idea when they see it; Middle Adopters (60 percent), who maintain the status quo unless given compelling reason to change; Late Adopters (18 percent), who will reluctantly accept change if the majority does; and Never Adopters (2 percent), who will spread ill will or leave if change occurs.[1]

The unfortunate reality is that most worship leaders are either Innovators or Early Adopters who have difficulty communicating with, or even understanding, the Middle Adopters who make up the bulk of the people in the pews. Perhaps this is why many attempts at introducing new music styles into the church are such resounding failures. Arn suggests that "the battle is for the Middlers." If Innovators can make vocal allies of the Early Adopters, it will go a long way toward tipping the balance of the Middlers in favor of experimenting with new worship expressions.

Most people are uncomfortable with change, so they need to be convinced of the value of change and assured that they will be included in the process. Many church members have huge emotional investments in their church's worship, and they may see innovation not as a creative response to the move of the Spirit as the Innovator does but as a grab for power by a faction within the church. This is especially true if the innovation pits older and younger generations against each other, as the introduction of new worship styles often does.

How can music ministers and other church leaders successfully navigate such hallowed yet thorny ground?

Prepare People for Change

Sow seeds. Before making any plans (or even discussions) public, it is essential to sow seeds informally throughout the congregation. Many music ministers discuss an idea with other church staff, receive the approval of the pastor, and then make the mistake of proceeding directly to the implementation stage. Even if all the official channels have been notified and approval has been given, the people in the pews may feel as if a coup has taken place and they are now worship fugitives. An only slightly better approach is to move from pastoral approval to a congregational forum. This may seem like a fine way to build community consensus about worship change, but it gives dissenters (Never Adopters) a platform to sow distrust and negatively sway those in the middle.

Instead, it is better to slowly build enthusiasm for change by identifying open-minded individuals from various groups within the church, spending time with them one-on-one, explaining the plan, and listening to their feedback. Based on these conversations, the music minister will be able to adapt the initiative to address concerns from a broad range of people and will gain allies throughout the church who can build support for the initiative within their circles. This kind of grassroots networking will lead to a sense of ownership among the congregation that will result in broad congregational support for change.

Two important points must be added to the above. First, any plan for building grassroots support for change presumes a relatively healthy congregation. If there are long-standing feuds between factions or the congregation is particularly strong-willed or self-centered, no amount of bridge-building will help the congregation reach consensus, and the resulting conflict will probably center around the music minister. Second, the Never Adopters, though a small group, can be extremely vocal. It is important to remain focused on the needs of the often silent majority rather than a vocal minority.

Use a trial period. Another method of easing the conflict that often surrounds worship change is using a trial period. People instinctively fear what they do not know, and worshipers are no different. In the same way that firsthand experience with other ethnicities is the best way to break down racial stereotypes and racism, a trial period gives worshipers firsthand experience with a worship innovation and will help break down their knee-jerk reactions to change.

Using a trial period also eases a congregation's decision-making process; rather than making an irrevocable decision, they are simply deciding to try something out. For instance, a church that is considering a shift from a traditional service to a blended service (composed of a mix of historic and modern worship elements) may test the new format during the summer when numbers are down and services are less formal anyway. A church that is moving beyond their sanctuary capacity may try holding two services during times of the year when capacity is highest—Christmas and Easter—to work out the kinks before changing to a multiple service format permanently.

The trial period also allows for feedback from the congregation. This feedback, which is based on the actual worship change rather than the perceived change, is very valuable for church leaders both in terms of logistics (i.e., "The worship team is great, but there are children's church teachers taking part; can we have them finish their music before the children are dismissed from the service?") and church unity ("The new music is fine, but having eight people with microphones filling up the platform creates a disparity between the new music and the hymns—could we move the people a bit to the side?").

Give permission to fail. Often, all that is needed to help a congregation transition into a new worship expression is to give them "permission to fail." That is not to say that the leaders expect a change not to work or encourage the people not to try. Instead, giving permission to fail lets people know that it's okay if they make mistakes. For example, when introducing a new song or style, use a short verbal introduction such as, "The next song is new, so please join in as soon as you're able." This creates a sense of camaraderie as the worshipers learn the song together. It changes the group consensus from "That was a flop" to "Pretty good for the first time."

Granted, a portion of the congregation is bound to be familiar with any worship element that is introduced. Is it still necessary to prepare the whole body? Yes, because doing so helps eliminate an insider/outsider mentality. For instance, an older woman once discussed with me the problems that the longtime members were having with the introduction of Praise & Worship. "It's not that we're against change," she elaborated, "but the lyrics printed in the bulletin are often different from what people are singing, we don't know when we're supposed to repeat songs or add echoes, and the young people all seem to know the songs already. We just end up feeling like outsiders in our own church."

Build slowly. A final caution for those who would introduce change, especially a new style of music, is to build slowly. The goal is not to become the hippest church in the shortest amount of time; the goal is to help your people worship in spirit and truth. Let the congregation gain confidence as they master new worship expressions, then build steadily on this foundation.

Attend to Details

The devil, they say, is in the details. Allowing an exciting worship initiative to be derailed by lack of attention to the necessary nuts-and-bolts preparations would be a shame.

Make Necessary Changes to Acoustics, Platform, and Sound System

Acoustics. Many older churches were built to accommodate the sound of the choir and organ, both of which benefit from long reverberation. Modern music favors dryer acoustics that allow the sound to be controlled through the sound system. To complicate things further, congregational singing needs lots of reflective surfaces in the immediate area of the singers or else they'll feel like they're the only ones singing. This is a difficult balance. Generally, a church should retain hard surfaces in the area of the congregation, put light rugs in the aisles, and add acoustically absorptive material to break up large areas of parallel walls. It is wise to consult an acoustician on these matters.

Platform. The platform area often needs to be modified to accommodate a worship team. Church architecture makes a statement about worship values, so it is important not to make unwitting theological statements when reconfiguring this space—replacing the baptismal font with a drum set, for instance. Instead, make room for the worship team—people, instruments, amps, and good sight lines—in an understated way that preserves the integrity of the worship space.

Sound system. Church sound systems are notorious epicenters of frustration, conflict, and failure. I can't tell you how many times I've had a worship team rendered useless due to a poor mix, set up the system myself due to tardy sound operators, or overhauled the sound system on my own time because of lack of church funds. I've even experienced feedback so excruciatingly loud that the musicians and congregation all stopped singing—covering their ears, instinctively ducking, and in some cases crying from the painful decibels. If the devil is in the details, many church sound systems are demon-possessed! I cannot say it emphatically enough: invest in a good sound system and train people to run it. Anything less guarantees the failure of the worship team and will provide enough distractions that worship will be adversely affected.

Funding. There are too many variables in church acoustics, platforms, and sound systems to make general recommendations, except these two: fund adequately and hire professionals. One time I was asked to recommend sound system changes to a church. I brought in a professional I trusted, and he auditioned his proposed system in the church one Sunday morning. The church leaders felt that it was a little too expensive (seven thousand dollars, which is actually a very modest system) and not quite perfect. After a number of other professional proposals had been rejected, one of the church members volunteered to install a system for six thousand dollars. The system proposed was more appropriate for a rock band or dance hall, and the church members had a collective heart attack when they arrived at church one Sunday morning to see two black speakers the size of small cars hanging from the walls of this historic landmark church. Not only that—the system didn't sound good! Over the next two years the speakers were replaced with a smaller model, and equalizers and feedback controllers were added to the original system. In the end, the "cheaper," volunteer-installed system cost two thousand dollars more than the original proposal. It was far less effective, and there was no one to call when things went wrong. I tell this story to convince you that sometimes you need to accept that, in the words of Psalm 139:6, "Such knowledge is too wonderful for me, too lofty for me to attain." Spend money on a professional acoustician, architect, or sound designer rather than letting well-intentioned volunteers make a mess of it.

Change Worship Order or Create a New Service if Needed

Many times, a new style of music can be easily inserted into a service—replace a hymn of adoration with a few praise songs, for instance. However, there are times when the worship service's structure must be adapted to accommodate either the logistics or the flow of the new music. I discuss this in chapter 4 in the section "Adapting Structure and Style."

In situations where the stylistic change is drastic—all the music will be in a new style or the change is expected to be controversial—a whole new service may be considered. Though church-growth experts encourage every new service to provide a new worship "menu item," I believe that multiple services in different music styles should be approached cautiously. Many churches try to convince themselves that a new service with a modern music style will reach the lost in their community when the real motive is to keep their own people from fighting over music, and the only "outreach" will be to members of other churches.

While there are many practical reasons to start a new service every time a new music style comes down the pike, I believe that the end result is disastrous. Where does it stop? The baby boomers' "contemporary" services have already become the "traditional" service in many evangelical churches, and Gen X is nipping at their heels with new worship styles—after all, doesn't each generation deserve to have their own service with their favorite music? Do we really want to encourage a church in which we wait for the older generation to die so we can move in with a new, exciting worship service? I hope not. I pray that the church of Jesus Christ will function as it's intended, with respect between generations, submission to one another (and their musical preferences) in love, and patience with change.

Work Out Logistical Details

Whether changing the worship order or creating a new service, there are a plethora of logistical details to consider: When will the worship team come on and off the platform? Do worship team members also sing in the choir or teach children's church, thus necessitating their finishing worship team duties by a certain time in the service? If a new service is created, will there be time between services to empty and refill the parking lot and sanctuary? Will multiple services in different formats affect Sunday school options (i.e., "I'd like to go to Sunday school X, but it's held during service Y")? What will be the ramifications of multiple services on musical volunteers?

Lyric Projection, Printing, and Licensing

New worship music requires new sources of music. This could mean adding a hymnal supplement to the pew or even purchasing a new hymnal, but it usually necessitates printing songs in a bulletin or projecting them on a screen. What is the best method? There is no correct answer, but there are issues to consider.

Using a hymnal, songbook, or hymnal supplement has the advantage of providing new music while feeling familiar to members who are used to singing from a hymnal. One person has remarked that with a hymnal, one can hold in their hands the church universal expressed musically, whereas projecting the lyrics on the screen gives the impression not of historic truths but a "trick of the light"—a momentary flash that is quickly replaced. Less philosophically, purchasing a printed book negates the need to pay licensing fees for each song. It also allows songs to be chosen on the spur of the moment—for instance, in response to something in a worship service or at a hymn sing. However, it restricts choices in the long term. Songs can be added to the repertoire one at a time if a projection screen or bulletin printing is used, but a hymnal or songbook locks in repertoire options for the life of the book.

Projecting lyrics on a screen gives the greatest flexibility, especially in modern music styles in which the repertoire changes rapidly. Many people argue that the projection screen causes people to lift their heads in a better singing posture, with their hands free to be more expressive in their worship. In some ways it is the most convenient option, and many churches are taking advantage of it. However, it is not a problem-free solution for every church. Projection screens are an eyesore. They may be positioned in ways that lessen their architectural impact, but in the end there will still be a large white screen invading the aesthetic of the sanctuary. Plus, they are extremely expensive, costing thousands of dollars for a modest system; you can buy a lot of hymnals and print a lot of bulletins for that price! It takes a good deal of labor to prepare a new presentation for each week's service. Projector systems also introduce a number of technical variables into the worship environment that can disrupt the singing: the slide operator may change slides too slowly or go to the wrong slide, the words of songs may be mistyped, or the computer may get a virus. When was the last time your hymnal malfunctioned?

Printing songs in the bulletin or on a song sheet is a third option, a compromise between the hymnal and projector. Like a hymnal it can be adjusted to each person's sight preferences—a significant problem with projectors if one is short or has bad eyesight. With the quality of today's photocopiers and scanners, music can be easily included in the bulletin, rather than just lyrics. And the bulletin can be read sequentially like a book, which enables worshipers to better understand the flow of the service. Like a projector it allows any song to be used, but it also requires time and effort to prepare.

Create a songbook. If you think weekly preparation and printing of lyrics is wasteful of church resources and harmful to the environment, you may want to consider making your own songbook. Many churches have in the pews a three-ring binder full of songs that the church uses regularly—when a new song enters the church's repertoire, it is simply inserted in the back of the songbook. Of course, the songbooks require a good deal of time to maintain and update.

Licensing music. If you project the lyrics, print them in a bulletin, or create a songbook, the law requires that you obtain a mechanical license to reproduce copyrighted songs. Essentially a mechanical license gives you permission to "publish" a song in the same way that permission is obtained for every song included in a hymnal.

It would be virtually impossible for every church to contact each song's publisher, draft a contract, and pay a fee. That's where licensing agencies step in. Churches can buy a cost-effective blanket license that allows the church to print or project thousands of songs. The licensing agency takes the churches' yearly fees and distributes them to the publishers and songwriters based on song usage reports from churches. Most songs in the Praise & Worship genre are covered by Christian Copyright Licensing Incorporated (www.ccli.com). Songs published by GIA, Hope, and other Catholic and denominational sources, including the music of Marty Haugen, John Bell, and Taizé, are covered by OneLicense.net (www.onelicense.net).

Licenses such as these cover only the reproduction of lyrics and music for congregational singing; they don't cover choral music, songbooks, or photocopying music for colleagues.

Form a Committee to Advise, Plan, and Gather Feedback

I'll be honest: I'm not a big fan of committee meetings. I have spent many hours sitting around a table, twirling my pencil impatiently, as the group process slows progress to a crawl. However, I have also been a "lone ranger" worship planner, and I know how dangerous it can be. A worship committee can give insight into how the congregation will react to particular worship changes, and they will be voices of reason when you're ready to charge into dangerous territory. They can also help the brainstorming and planning process—if two heads are better than one, imagine four or eight! The members of the committee can exponentially extend the music minister's reach, gathering feedback from every corner of the congregation. Finally, a worship committee offers a certain amount of protection, distributing the heat when things go wrong. If there is no worship committee in your church, form one.

2

ASSEMBLING THE TEAM

Recruiting

Rare is the person who has excellent musical skills, vibrant faith, and the ability to collaborate with others. Even more rare is finding a full team of musicians like this. Planning and patience will allow you to assemble the best team possible in your situation.

Team Structure

Before recruiting begins, you must know the type of person you are looking for. Begin by building the core of the team.

Pianist. Most fundamental to the team's musical structure is the pianist. The piano is not only one of the backbone instruments of the worship team, it is also one of the most versatile. This is especially important in a blended worship setting where the piano can be a bridge between Praise & Worship and other forms of worship. Therefore it is important to find a pianist who can improvise from a leadsheet, read music from a score, transpose, and hopefully sight-read like a fiend. (This goal is ideal. For suggestions when it is not possible, see "Assembling the Team in a Small Church," p. 48.) I don't know how many times I've been in the situation where the pastor asks for a different closing song on the spur of the moment, or an event like September 11 takes place and makes the planned praise set suddenly inappropriate. At times like this, a pianist you can trust is worth his or her weight in gold.

Rhythm section. Besides the piano, a full worship team needs guitar, bass, and drums to round out the rhythm section. The specific roles each of these instruments plays are fleshed out in more detail in chapter 5, "Making Music." Simply put, you should look for a guitarist with solid strum and pick patterns, a bassist who keeps impeccable time, and a drummer who can play sensitively (i.e., softly when needed). Of course, these instruments can and should do much more than this, but these are their most essential roles when playing in a church setting. Once this core rhythm section is established, other instruments such as electric guitar, saxophone, violin, and hand percussion can be added as available.

Vocalists. In most situations, you will discover a glut of female singers who are interested in singing with the worship team. I have no idea why gender roles are so clearly defined on worship teams, but it seems that nine times out of ten all the singers will be female and all the instrumentalists will be male. This creates two problems: first, having too many women throws off the balance of vocal harmonies; second, it creates the impression that praising God is a "woman thing." Even if you can't achieve a perfect balance of male and female singers, aim to have at least a few men singing with the worship team. Men in the congregation often sing timidly, and having male role models up front may give them the confidence they need to sing out.

Whether male or female, the singers should have pleasant but not necessarily exceptional voices. Most important is their ability to blend. The Mariah Carey wannabes may sound impressive at first, but you will soon tire of trying to tame their soloistic approach. Optimally, worship team singers should be able to read music and improvise harmonies. Also, because the singers are often the members of the team to connect with the congregation verbally, it is important that at least some of your vocalists feel comfortable praying, reading Scripture, and making verbal transitions.

Room for growth. Finally, it is important that your team structure allows for the growth and mentoring of younger or inexperienced musicians. If we truly view our worship teams as ministries, we need to do more than simply assemble the best team to get the job done. We need to foster the growth and discovery of gifts of those under our care—this is the difference between *using* and *nurturing* the musicians God has given us.

The worship team structure can encourage the growth of musicians in a number of ways. You may choose to have yearly auditions; this gives new musicians a point of entry and allows your old musicians a chance to take a periodic sabbatical. You can pair an experienced musician on a core instrument with an inexperienced musician on an auxiliary instrument—for example, a piano with a keyboard. This builds musical mentoring into the fabric of the team, with inexperienced players learning songs and techniques alongside a better player. If enough musicians are available, you can create an "A Team" and a "B Team." This gives the musicians of the church more opportunities to participate and allows the "A Team" a rest once in a while.

Another means of allowing for growth of the church's musicians is evaluating the role the music minister plays. In many situations the music minister also leads the worship team from the piano or guitar. While this is the most efficient way to lead the team, it can create a situation in which the rest of the musicians form a backup band rather than a team. It is the difference between a leader-centered team and a leader-directed team. On the leader-centered team, the leader sings, plays, handles musical transitions, and speaks to the congregation while the rest of the musicians follow along; on the leader-directed team, all musicians are free to use and develop the gifts that God has given them at the appropriate time. On a leader-centered team, the leader is the focus and runs the danger of becoming an idol to the congregation; on the leader-directed team, the focus is distributed among the musicians, which tends to create a sense of shared purpose in worship between leader, team, and congregation.

Sometimes it is just a matter of balance. For instance, because my worship teams at Northwestern College were new each year, I often took a more prominent role at the beginning of the year when we needed to get up and running quickly. Then, as I discovered each musician's gifts, I handed over more and more leadership to the team members; by the end of the year, they led worship without my assistance.

Advertising

Music ministers are often uncomfortable with things like advertising; it just seems unspiritual to use a business technique to draw musicians rather than relying on the Holy Spirit to woo them. Surely prayer must saturate the process, but I believe that taking a businesslike approach to advertising—and even auditions—can help create an open atmosphere in which everyone feels that they have equal opportunity to take part in the church's worship leadership. You may hope to avoid hurting people's feelings by simply inviting the musicians you want to join the team, but those musicians who aren't invited will feel that they have been barred from an exclusive club.

Instead, it is best to advertise any positions on the worship team as widely as possible within the church. This open-door policy helps the music minister avoid any accusations of favoritism and will hopefully draw excellent new musicians into the ministry. Yes, it will create a painful situation when you have to turn some away, but this is all part of the discernment process for the team and the person as they both seek to discover their part in God's work.

Advertising widely does not preclude word-of-mouth suggestions. The fact is that many musicians will not respond to a notice in the church newsletter, but they will to a friend's nudging. If you need a musician for a team, don't be shy. Spread the word to the people on your teams and in the church and ask them to suggest likely candidates. I have found my "rat on a friend" program to be a useful recruiting tool. Every time I advertise for musicians, I make it clear that anonymous nominations will be accepted—which usually results in a few shy spouses or friends becoming involved in the music ministry.

Faith Issues

Eventually, you will ask the question "Should I include non-Christians on my worship team?" The definitive answer is "Maybe."

Naturally, the ideal is that every person involved in worship is an outstanding musician who has a mature, contagious faith in Christ. But in the real world, Billy Graham doesn't play guitar. And in your local church you will often be approached by a musician who would like to take part in the music ministry even though they are not strong in their faith. Should this seeker be involved in worship leadership? Here are some rules of thumb:

The more focused the position, the more important the person's faith. It is clear that the pastor's faith is more important than the sound operator's in guiding the spiritual life of a church. Though they are both contributing essential elements to the ministry, the pastor has direct access to the congregation. In the same way, a lead singer on a worship team has a position of focused leadership—this "lead worshiper" must be a mature Christian who is ready to respond to the Spirit, lead the congregation in song and prayer, and be an example of a vibrant Christian life. He or she must be much more than a good singer. However, a bass player or drummer doesn't have the same level of connection with the congregation, and perhaps a person with more music skills than spiritual depth can fill this role.

The involvement of a non-Christian should do the person more good than it does the team harm. There was once a girl in my church who we'll call Shannon, because that was her name. She was the girlfriend of one of my singers and wanted to join the choir. Though she was a nice, moral girl, I knew she wasn't a Christian. I talked to my pastor, and we decided to let her sing. After about two years singing with the choir, she called to see if she could stop by my office. "Stopping by the office" is usually a euphemism for "I'm really upset about something" or "I'm quitting," so I was nervous. O me of little faith! When she stopped by, she sat down and said, "I've given my life to the Lord, and I'm going to be baptized. I wanted you to be the first to know." I was absolutely thrilled to know that her involvement in the choir had given her a chance to hear the Word, experience authentic worship, and observe the faith of ordinary Christians week after week—and subsequently come to faith in Christ.

If someone wants to take part in worship, it probably means that they are open to the gospel. Giving them a chance to participate in a music ministry is often a point of entry into the faith. Of course,

I wouldn't want a significant percentage of non-Christians in the ministry, but a handful of seekers will benefit by being a part of a community of faith.

Non-Christians must be willing to adhere to the same "lifestyle" expectations as the rest of the team. It is one thing to allow a seeker to take a low profile role in a church's worship leadership, but it is another to exempt them from the expectations you have for the rest of your team. Nothing does more harm to a music ministry's morale than to expect a lifestyle of sexual purity from your musicians while one of the members is openly living with a partner. The same is true of drinking or any other guideline that your team members follow. When you talk to a prospective team member, make your expectations clear, especially if you intuit that it may be an issue.

Don't make the decision alone. The decision to include or exclude a potential worship team member based on their faith (or lack of it) is extremely difficult. Therefore, it is wise not to make the decision alone. If you are a music minister or worship team leader, consult your pastor. If you are a pastor, consult your elders. Above all, pray for the Lord's guidance as you seek to create an inclusive community of worshipers and seekers.

Interviewing

Pros and Cons of Auditions

Auditions are a controversial topic. Some think that the people of the church should be allowed to take part in any ministry they choose, and that auditions for worship teams unnecessarily exclude those who want to praise God. They think that auditions create hard feelings for those who aren't chosen, bringing ill will toward the music ministry in general. After all, isn't true worship about what's in the heart rather than one's musical ability?

On the other side there are those who affirm the audition process because it helps the worship team leader get to know each musician's skills. It also sets a precedent for quality—shouldn't a church offer its best in worship? Finally, they argue that it helps people discern their gifts. To allow a marginal musician into a worship team might rob the Sunday school of a teacher, and more important it keeps them from finding their true calling within the body of believers.

Both sides have valid points. It is important to try to set the bar high for an excellent worship team while also fostering a loving and affirming community. Not an easy task. One compromise is to move away from auditions à la *American Idol,* and move toward worship team *interviews.* First of all, the word *interview* doesn't sound as intimidating as *audition.* It also emphasizes the fact that the team is looking for not only quality musicianship but also spiritual maturity and ability to work on a team.

Application Materials

The foundation of a positive interview experience is robust application materials. Even though it takes some time to create, distribute, and process an interview packet, it is worth the trouble. Potential team members will have fewer questions, less fear about walking into their interview, and more confidence that the process will be fair. Interviewers will glean a good deal of background information that will allow them to better use the interview time. Further, a standardized interview packet will help even the playing field, minimizing the effects or appearance of favoritism. Application materials should include the following:

Description of worship team/s, available positions, and expected commitment. The first thing prospective team members should see is a clear description of the teams, who should apply, and what will be expected of them if they are asked to join a team. It wastes everyone's time to interview an accordion player if you're forming an alternative rock worship team for a youth service. (Personally, I've always wanted to have an accordion on my worship team, but none have been forthcoming.) Create an information sheet that answers questions applicants may have:

How many worship teams are there?
How many musicians on each team?
What style of music do they play?

In which services do they lead?

What instruments are you seeking?

Will you consider instruments not on the list?

Are these paid or volunteer positions?

How often will the team practice and lead worship?

What equipment does the church provide (drums, amps, keyboard)?

Whom should they call if they have a question?

Explanation of the interview process. Nothing fosters fear more than the unknown. Tell applicants exactly what to expect during the interview process:

When are applications due?

When are the interviews?

Where can they sign up for an interview time?

What will they be asked to do at the interview (in detail)?

Should they still apply if they're weak in sight-reading or improvising chords?

When will decisions be made?

Application form. The application form is your opportunity to gather background information, find out about a musician's faith, and ask questions that can provide a starting point for interview discussions. Of course, the application must ask for basic information such as name, phone, email, address, and instrument or voice part. But this is also your chance to probe deeper into the prospective musician's experience and priorities:

What is your background as a Christian, musician, and/or worship leader?

If you were on a team previously, how did you grow through the experience, and what fresh quality will you bring to this team?

Why do you want to be on a team?

What are one or two unique qualities or gifts you will bring to the team?

If you are chosen for a team, in which area would you most like to grow or develop?

What will you do if you are not chosen?

Scenario: Your worship team leader chooses you to perform a solo part, and you feel that the choice is based more on your close friendship with the leader than your abilities as a worship leader. Even more difficult, you know that another deserving musician on the team is frustrated by lack of opportunities. What would you do? (Sometimes questions like this give insight into how the applicant relates to authority and fellow musicians.)

If you were stranded on a desert island, what *one* CD would you want to have with you? (Use this one to find out what the person's musical influences are.)

If you could be any vegetable, what would it be? Why? (Just for fun. . . .)

The trick is to ask questions that don't allow the applicant to answer the "right" way. Most applicants will write, "I want to join a team because I love the Lord and love to worship him, and I want to use my musical talents to glorify his name." (What applicant is going to write, "I'm a lukewarm Christian looking for a place to jam and meet girls"?) Try to uncover unique information to use as a springboard during your interview time. ("I see that your 'desert island' CD is Moby's 'Play'; do you play synthesizer and sampler as well as piano?")

Song/s to learn for interview. Any music that applicants need to learn for the interview should be included in the application packet with clear instructions. For example, a leadsheet may include these instructions:

Vocalists, learn the melody and work out a harmony part in your range.

Pianists, be prepared to play chords and melody.

Guitarists, be able to strum and fingerpick the chords, preferably while singing the melody.

Bassists and drummers, be prepared to play your parts along with a pianist and guitarist.

Interview Process

The goal of the interview is not to weed out the weak but to help people discover their gifts in an affirming atmosphere.

Assemble a panel of interviewers. Include at least three people on the interview panel. Each person will contribute his or her own unique perspective to the interview decisions, making the process as equitable as possible. Create the interview panel from leaders who will be significantly affected by interview decisions. It may be wise to include the music minister, key musicians, the pastor, or the elder who oversees the worship committee.

Prepare for interviews. The most important way of preparing for the interview process is prayer. Pray that the Lord would give interviewees peace, interviewers wisdom, and all discernment about the use of their gifts in the kingdom. Fasting before the interviews is also appropriate; ask the Lord for clarity during the process. I have always been surprised at how quickly consensus emerges when a panel of interviewers fasts and prays before the interview process.

Make sure the interview room is comfortable and ready for interviews. Avoid arranging the room like an interrogation cell; try setting up chairs in a cozy circle or semicircle instead. Don't place the interviewees so far away from the interviewers that they feel isolated but not so close that they feel intimidated. Have paper and pencils available for interviewers and music ready for the interviewees on a music stand or piano. Think through any additional details that will help you optimize your interview time: Do you need someone outside the interview room to send musicians in when you're ready for them? Will any of the musicians need an amp or drum set? Have you read applications before the interview and prepared questions for each applicant?

Chosen song. Beginning the interview by letting applicants present a song with which they are most comfortable puts them at ease. Have them arrive prepared to do one song of their choice in any style that flatters their voice or instrument. This is not only a chance to put the applicant at ease but an opportunity to find out the style and repertoire with which they are most comfortable. This is also a good time to observe their basic vocal quality or instrumental skill level.

Prepared song. Once they've had a chance to warm up with a song of their choosing, proceed to the song that was included in the interview packet. Part of the reason for having everyone prepare the same song for the interview is to give you a chance to compare apples to apples. Therefore it is best if the prepared song is not well known. It is also good to choose a song with a somewhat neutral music style so that no one has an advantage.

The prepared song often uncovers the important issue of the applicant's work ethic. Musicians who arrive with the song thoroughly learned show that they are able to practice efficiently—an important skill for a musician who often has to learn as much as thirty minutes of music every week. Unfortunately, many show up for the interview with little mastery of the song they've been asked to prepare. I even had one applicant make up a song loosely based on the words of the required song, a creative and amusing solution to a lack of preparation. One can't assume musicians will magically gain practice skills if put on a team—bring them into the music ministry at your own risk!

The prepared song is also a good opportunity to see how well the applicant responds to directions. Just as you would in an actual rehearsal setting, ask the interviewee to change the style they're using or try a different technique. For example, with a pianist you might ask, "I hear this as more of a ballad—could you slow it down and smooth it out?" Or, "Let's pretend we're going into the last verse, which will be soft and sparse—why don't you do some harp-like arpeggios in the upper octave; now slowly build to the last chorus." You may want to ask a vocalist to improvise or read a harmony line rather than sing the melody, or you could ask a guitarist to try a different strum or fingerpick pattern.

All these requests give insight into the breadth of the musician's technique and how able (or willing) they are to adapt their style for the sake of the team's sound. For instance, I once had a singer who, for her prepared song, sang an improvised alto line. I told her that she sang harmony beautifully and asked her to sing the melody, to which she responded, "I sing alto." I assured her she had made it clear that she could sing an alto line very well but I was really interested in hearing her sing the melody. "But this is what I do," she said. "I make up harmonies in the alto range." I'm still not sure if her response meant, "I don't know how to sing a melody" or, "I refuse to sing anything but my own alto lines"; in either case, she didn't strike me as very adaptable.

Sight-reading. The final musical section of the interview is not only a chance to hear how well the applicant sight-reads but also a way to explore remaining areas of their musicianship. I usually start by having them read a rhythmic praise song. If they're a vocalist, it shows how well they read syncopations and fast-moving pitches. For instrumentalists it shows a different style of playing; this is especially true for pianists, who are usually more comfortable playing ballads than upbeat songs with a band.

Next, explore musical styles or techniques using appropriate sight-reading examples. Ask them to read a hymn. Request that they play a familiar song in different styles. Have them change chords from the written leadsheet or use a particular rhythmic hit in the song. See if they can modulate and transpose.

The point is not to continue challenging them until they fail; it is to fully explore their existing musical gifts as well as their potential for growth. My rule of thumb is to push the better musicians harder in their interview. If an interviewee has done poorly on both their chosen song and the song that they've prepared, it isn't kind or sensible to continue to request things that they obviously can't do; just thank them and move on. However, if an interviewee shows real promise, take the opportunity to fully explore their gifts. If you already have a brilliant acoustic guitarist on a team, find out how well the interviewee plays electric guitar. If a young musician shows potential, explore how quickly they learn and how eager they are to improve.

Put them at ease and help them shine. It's hard to put yourself in the interviewee's shoes; *you* know that the interview will be a comfortable affair led by friendly people, but they don't. Give each interviewee a warm smile and friendly greeting, leading them to the place you'd like them to stand and letting them know when you're ready to begin. You can't necessarily take away their nervousness, but you certainly don't want to contribute to it! Remember that each person is affected by nerves differently—some shake or mumble, others appear overconfident, some will even become belligerent; try to allow some slack for nervous behavior.

The best way to put interviewees at ease is to show them that you are interested in helping them shine rather than tripping them up. If they have a technical glitch, assure them that everyone makes mistakes. If they can't do something you ask, ask them to do something else. For example, if a pianist doesn't do well reading chord charts, have them try reading from piano music. If they don't excel at one style, try another. If a singer is having problems with intonation, have them sing in a different range to explore their voice; many times I have had "altos" leave their interviews excited to have discovered that they are budding sopranos!

Questions. Finally, ask the interviewee one or two questions to get to know them better. I find it useful to highlight interesting or questionable information on their application form prior to the interview and ask questions based on that. For example, "You said on your form that you led worship teams during college; would you be interested in leading a team in the future?" Or, "You mention a 'difficult time of life in which worship played a pivotal role in strengthening your faith'; could you talk more specifically about that experience and how that affects your approach to leading worship today?"

Before the interview ends, ask the interviewee if they have any questions. Thank them for applying and let them know when they can expect to hear from you.

How to Evaluate Interviewees

When I worked at Northwestern College, over sixty students tried out for four worship teams every fall. It was no easy task to hear this many students for ten to fifteen minutes each, remember every one, evaluate them fairly, and place them on the team that best matched their skills. Your interviews may not be as extensive as this, but you will still benefit from using some of these interview techniques.

Take copious notes. Jot down a physical description, the songs they sang, or some phrase that will jog your memory about the applicant later—something like "red-haired, left-handed guitarist who played 'Smoke on the Water.'" Make notes about interviewees and their performance, such as "seems to lack confidence," "pitch was shaky in his low register," or "great harmonies." Write down particular strengths or weaknesses they would bring to a group: "reads hymns well, but only rudimentary ability with chord charts." If they are trying out for different ensembles, note which group they would fit in. Finally, interviewers should rate each person on the same scale. You may feel uncomfortable assigning a person a number, but this is a useful tool when discussing candidates later.

Look for particular skills. Go into the interviews knowing what skills you value in each instrument and any particular needs your teams may have.

Vocalists: evaluate pitch, tone, diction, and stage presence. Would you be encouraged to worship if they were leading?

Pianists: how well do they sight-read, play chord charts, or adapt to different music styles? Would the person make a solid backbone to an ensemble?

Guitarists: do they know open and barre chords? Do they have solid strumming and fingerpicking technique and a good sense of rhythm? Can they solo? Do they play everything in one style, or can they adapt to each song?

Bassists: can they read a chord chart, including inversions? Do they lock in with the drum and guitar? Do they play musically?

Drummers: can they vary their dynamics and adapt their music style? Do they listen to the others in the ensemble? Do they play hand percussion?

Flutists, violinists, or other ancillary instrumentalists: do they read music and improvise interesting lines that complement a song's arrangement? Do they sing harmony, play synthesizer, or have some other skill that would expand their usefulness to the worship team?

Are there particular holes in the worship team/s that you hope to fill? For example, a longtime pianist may be taking a year off, and you need to find a replacement. During the interviews keep an eye out for pianists who could assume this role, and fully explore the skills of likely candidates. Perhaps you plan to have one of your teams lead a new, more progressive service and you want an electric guitarist to join the team. If an acoustic guitarist shows promise, ask if they own an electric guitar and then explore that side of their playing in more depth.

Make decisions. Final decisions about who should be included or excluded from the worship team are often excruciatingly difficult. I find it helpful to create an index card for each interviewee and lay all the cards on a large table, allowing the interview panel to visualize the decision process. First, arrange the cards by instrument or voice part. Next, create a pile for each team. Usually, there will be immediate consensus about a small percentage of the musicians: "She is the perfect drummer for this team," or "He has to be a tenor on that team." With these foundational musicians in place, you can start filling in the rest of the team. These are often the most difficult decisions because there are only subtle differences between the musicians.

Some factors that may affect your decisions are the compatibility of the musicians' personalities and the blend of their voices or playing style. Ideally, the worship team should have musicians of similar skill levels, although sometimes it is fine to include a few weaker musicians who will grow by interacting with more experienced musicians. Reputation is another important factor. Many times discussions of a particular musician have uncovered that he or she has a history of causing problems in other areas of the church; or a person with less musical skill is placed on a team because of their reputation as a loving and faithful follower of Christ.

There is no foolproof method of placing musicians with teams. Continue to pray. Keep moving index cards into various configurations until the best pattern emerges.

Follow-up Letter or Call

Regardless of the outcome of the interview, everyone who applied deserves to receive a phone call or letter. If they have been chosen for a team, congratulations and information about rehearsals are in order. If they weren't chosen for a team, communicate the news to them sensitively. Thank them for interviewing. Remind them that many factors go into these decisions, many of which have nothing to do with skill. Encourage them to continue to seek ways to use their gifts, perhaps including information about other areas of ministry in the church.

Only discuss weaknesses that were apparent in their interview if asked. Most people will find it insulting to hear, "We didn't choose you for a team because your pitch is weak." However, an interviewee who sincerely wants to improve may ask for feedback, at which point it would be helpful to give them details about your decision. Your critique should always be constructive and loving, softened by a sincere compliment: "You have a beautiful voice, but we didn't think that your music-reading was strong enough for you to keep up with the amount of music this team has to learn every week. Perhaps some voice or piano lessons could help you focus on your sight-reading skills."

Rejection is difficult, whether you're on the receiving or giving end. The process is much easier if you truly believe that the Lord has given each of his followers unique gifts, and that the worship team interview is only one step in a person's journey of discerning these gifts. Assist interviewees on their journey by being prayerful, kind, and honest.

Assembling the Team in a Small Church

Many churches simply don't have the resources for the recruiting process that is described here. Several of these principles can be adapted to your unique situation. For example, the interview might be as low-key as a one-on-one "get to know you" session or inviting candidates to rehearse with an existing team for a night. Though this process can be trimmed and adapted, two principles should remain: assembling the best team possible and helping people discern their gifts.

Some churches may need to consider prayerfully hiring a few key musicians from outside the church. For example, if you have a complete worship team except for a guitarist, hiring this musician would enable the church's musicians to lead more effectively until a guitarist is available from inside the church. Other churches may find that it is a worthwhile investment to pay for a church member's music lessons to enable them to contribute to the team.

Establishing a New Worship Team

The interviews are over, the decisions have been made, and an eager new team is awaiting its first rehearsal. What do you do now? You may be anxious to jump right into rehearsals, but it's better to take the time to lay the groundwork for the team's long-term health. As you can imagine, establishing ground rules for the team members before they begin rehearsing is much easier than changing team expectations a year down the road.

Characteristics of Worship Teams

Before establishing team ground rules, you must understand the worship team's unique environment. The worship team is an odd mix of prayer circle, church choir, and garage band. It's this blend of elements that makes working with worship teams so invigorating . . . and so frustrating. I wish I could say that I'm a master of worship team relations, but I'm still learning what successful leadership looks like in this challenging environment.

Heterogeneous music group. Relating to a choir is relatively simple. There are two parties, the conductor and the singers, and though there may be one hundred singers they all share the same task. Relating to an orchestra is perhaps a bit more complex because the musicians are playing different instruments, but there is still essentially two-way communication between conductor and orchestra, mediated through the printed music. The worship team, on the other hand, is not only a collection of different instruments; it is a group of musicians with fundamentally different skills and totally different approaches who need radically different types of information during rehearsal. When the worship team leader tells the singers to enunciate a phrase more clearly, it has no bearing on the task of the drummer. The heterogeneous makeup of the worship team creates complex lines of communication. Rather than the two-way communication of the choir rehearsal, the worship team is a tangled web of communication between the leader and the musicians, and between the musicians themselves.

Improvised music style. Traditional music ensembles use printed music, so their rehearsals have a very clear goal—learn the notes. However, worship teams normally play "off the page." They may use music as a starting point, but the musicians will soon contribute their own musical lines that bear their unique personal imprint. An alto in a traditional choir would never suggest an improvement to Fauré's written alto line, but in a worship team vocalists often suggest new harmonies. The rhythm section has even greater ability to change the music based on their personal contributions: they may suggest using a hip-hop beat or a walking bass line. Sometimes these unique contributions are not conscious decisions. I once worked with a drummer who had only three or four different drum beats. I could interpret a song any way I wanted as long as it fit one of those beats!

Personality differences. The worship team setting is intimate, so personality differences tend to be quite pronounced. Some worship team members will be "worker bees"—hardworking team players who are content to contribute their talents in any way they can. Others are prima donnas, craving the sanctified spotlight of the worship team. (People over thirty who still want to be in a rock-and-roll band have only two options: wedding reception bands and worship teams.) There is also a difference between "head" and "heart" types of people. The "head" team members want to get down to business, whereas the "heart" people want time to bond with the other team members. Conflict can ensue over this difference of approach as it did in one of my worship teams: the singers would stop to discuss their feelings about the songs, the harmonies, how things went the previous week, or any other subject about which one could have feelings. Eventually, when the drummer could take no more, he would interrupt their conversation with a sarcasm-drenched comment such as, "I'd really like to hang around and talk about my feelings, but some of us have to get up for work in the morning."

Different spiritual approaches. Some people approach the worship team as they would any other ensemble, but others view it as a special spiritual experience—a musical "holy of holies." Perhaps this is due to Praise & Worship's charismatic roots. In any case, there is often a disparity between charismatic and non-charismatic worship team members. Charismatic members will push for longer praise sets and an ecstatic leadership style, whereas the non-charismatic members will be more conservative in their approach. This can lead to friction on the team, with the charismatic members feeling tethered by tradition, church authority, and congregational expectations, and the non-charismatic members being stretched beyond their comfort zone.

All these differences built into the fabric of the worship team result in a complex rehearsal environment. At their worst, worship team rehearsals reach a level of chaos that would make a junior high youth group leader blanch: while you're trying to clean up a transition with the pianist, the bass and drummer are jamming, the singers are catching up with each other, the electric guitarist is practicing Van Halen licks, and the acoustic guitarist is praying for the soul of the electric guitarist. At their best, worship teams can enjoy invigorating collaboration in which each musician brings his or her unique gift, fostering loving relationships that lead to a meaningful sense of community.

Setting Ground Rules

The key to fostering the positive aspects of the worship team's characteristics while diminishing the inherent problems is to make the team members' responsibilities clear from the beginning.

Length of commitment. This may have been addressed during the interview, but reiterating it is wise. Make it clear that by choosing a person for the team, you have made a commitment to them; in return, you expect a commitment from them. Put a time limit on that commitment, giving both parties a chance to reevaluate their priorities at the end of the commitment period.

Attendance. Some team members have an ingrained sense of duty that compels them to be at every rehearsal and worship service, while others will forget or simply decide that something more interesting has come up. You must make your attendance expectations clear from the beginning. What are acceptable reasons for being absent? Business out of town? Sickness? Birthday parties and ball games? Is rehearsal attendance as important as worship attendance? (My answer is yes.) If team members will be absent on Sunday, should they still attend rehearsal? If they are going to be absent, how far in advance do they need to tell you? (I provide a sign-out sheet for this purpose.) What are the repercussions of poor attendance?

Punctuality. I once had two singers who were constantly tardy. They would meander into rehearsal fifteen to thirty minutes late. On Sundays they would show up at church at the appointed time, but by the time they had their music ready, had been sidetracked talking to people, and had visited the bathroom, they were late for the warm-up. One Sunday I had finally had enough. The team had already run through all the music and completed the sound check without these two latecomers, so when they sauntered into the sanctuary I informed them that they were too late to sing that day. My tone must have been pretty icy, because that day became known as "Spanking Sunday."

That scene may have been avoided if I had made my expectations more clear. When do rehearsals start? Is everybody needed for warm-up and sound check? Should the musicians *arrive* at the start time, or be *set up and ready to play* by the start time? Who is responsible for setting up various items—will church instruments such as keyboard and drums be set up by the player, the sound team, or the director? Are vocalists responsible for any setup? Do the musicians help set up the sound system?

Of course, punctuality is the director's responsibility as well. It is unreasonable to demand that your musicians arrive on time if you don't. It's also unfair to expect punctuality at the beginning of rehearsal if you are not punctual about ending it. Being punctual is a way of respecting and valuing others. I have found that the best cure for tardiness is to model punctuality for the team: set up equipment well before rehearsal, have stands and music prepared for each person, allow fifteen minutes before rehearsal to greet people as they arrive, and start promptly with prayer. If you value punctuality, your team will as well.

Team structure. Imagine the scenario: your drummer suggests that you play a particular song faster, like she's heard it on a particular CD. You tell her no and continue rehearsal, wondering if she's trying to undermine your leadership: you planned the set of songs—why does she always need to question (criticize?) everything? Meanwhile, she's hurt because she feels that either you didn't listen to her idea or you're just so full of yourself that you're never willing to listen to anyone's ideas.

The collaborative nature of the worship team often diminishes the authority of the leader. In a choir setting, the conductor is a "benevolent dictator," but worship teams can easily become democracies or even anarchies. The worship team leader shouldn't seek power for power's sake but needs to be willing to accept the responsibility and authority that comes with leadership. This leadership can take many different forms, but it needs to be communicated to the team. Explain how rehearsal communication should work: Should the musicians discuss things among themselves or only ask you? Do you want creative input from the musicians? How much? At what point in the process? Establishing how the team will collaborate helps avoid power struggles and miscommunications.

Unity. Musicians are notoriously prone to jealousy, ego wars, and backbiting. The whole team must fight those instincts, dedicating themselves instead to love, support, and unity. Never speak negatively about a team member in front of them or to others, and expect the same from your team. Affirm each member and encourage them to rejoice with each other over their successes rather than harboring resentment or jealousy. If a conflict arises, follow Jesus's model and approach that person directly (Matt. 18:15–20). Insist that your team does the same with you and each other.

Lifestyle and church expectations. Most churches have conduct expectations for their church members and leaders. These expectations, often unspoken, include everything from prohibiting homosexual behavior to insisting on involvement in a Bible study. Make sure these expectations are clear to your worship team members, especially those who are new to the church. Verbalizing the expectation that team members will be sexually pure may be awkward, but it will be even more difficult a year down the road when you find out that one of your singers is living with his girlfriend!

Appearance. Because the worship team is visible to the whole congregation, it may be important to your church leaders that the team dresses in a particular fashion. Usually the unwritten dress code focuses on two areas: avoiding provocative clothing and wearing appropriately dressy attire. Both of these areas depend on the particular church. In one, "provocative" may mean a woman wearing pants, in another "nice" clothes may indicate a polo shirt and khakis. If you make your dress expectations clear from the beginning, you will save yourself the embarrassment of having to talk to a musician about her short skirt or explaining to a team member why the pastor wants him to wear a tie.

It may seem like nit-picking to start a new team or new year with a list of things they can and can't do, but clearly explaining the team's ground rules will provide boundaries, which the members will appreciate (even if they disagree with some of the points). It is even helpful to put the list of expectations in writing so there is no question about it later on. I have gone so far as to put it in the form of a contract, so that when things start to get lax in the middle of the year or there is a conflict over a particular issue, I can remind the team what they agreed to from the beginning. For existing teams that have no clear expectations or are experiencing conflict over responsibilities and relations, I have found it helpful to have them create their own ground rules. They will come up with ground rules that foster respect and discipline, and they will be more likely to support rules that they created themselves.

3

BUILDING REPERTOIRE

Repertoire Is Theology

"Well, you pick some upbeat praise songs, and I'll take care of the theology," the pastor said. In a moment, it became crystal clear that he and I had vastly different ideas about the role of congregational singing in spiritual formation. To him, the music is a warm-up to the real spiritual meat of the sermon. To me, congregational singing puts the Christian faith on the tongues of the people, letting it work its way down to the soul.

The issue is not whether preaching or music is more effective at shaping faith; it is an issue of creating a church environment that allows people to grow in faith through enculturation. Enculturation is the development of behaviors that one "catches" rather than learns. Every day we are surrounded by subtle messages that inform our beliefs and actions on a subconscious level; these messages are often more powerful than direct messages we hear from parents, teachers, and society. Therefore, when a youth group leader tells a teen to abstain from having sex before marriage, he or she is combating thousands of messages that the teen has already received from TV and movies that tell the teen that people who are in love have sex regardless of their marital status.

In the same way that deep-seated values are "caught" in the larger culture, faith values can be caught in worship. The wise pastor and worship planner consider not only the immediate impact of a worship service but the long-term messages that are being reinforced week after week through sermons, music, and Scripture readings. A service built around the theme "Raising Teens without Raising Your Blood Pressure" (a service I experienced) may provide some immediately helpful hints for parents, but if this type of service is the weekly diet, what does it teach? That God exists to make you calm and successful? That the Bible is a divine self-help manual? Instead, leaders should think of the congregation as a "tree planted by the waters," planning worship that will sustain slow, long-term growth. For the music minister, the goal of providing long-range sustenance means focusing on not only finding a song to match the sermon theme each week but building repertoire over time that paints a broad and deep picture of God and the Christian life.

Analyzing Repertoire

In order to understand the enculturated picture of God that is being promoted through the worship music, the worship planner must assess the church's existing repertoire. The most systematic and beneficial method of assessing repertoire is to categorize each song according to its content and function, analyzing the patterns that emerge. The following are various ways of categorizing songs that will help you objectively analyze your church's repertoire.

Line of Communication

Who is speaking to whom in the songs we sing? We may reflexively assume that the worshiper is always speaking to God, but this is not the case.[1]

Human to human. Numerous congregational songs speak horizontally (human to human), often exhorting one another to enter into worship, such as Brian Doerksen's "Come, Now Is the Time to Worship."

Human to God. Other songs use a vertical voice, sung directly from the worshiper to God. They address the Lord as "You" rather than "He" and include songs of adoration such as "Worthy, You Are Worthy" by Don Moen and "Here I Am to Worship" by Tim Hughes.

God to human. Another line of communication is revelation, or God speaking to humans. In revelation songs, God speaks directly in first person as found in the verses of "Here I Am, Lord" by Dan Schutte, or more generally through the words of Scripture. Reformed churches will want to pay particular attention to this category, as it is the backbone of their revelation and response worship pattern.

Other. There are other possible lines of communication in worship songs such as *humans to other beings* (e.g., "All Creatures of Our God and King"), as well as songs in which the *worshiper speaks to himself or herself.* However, the latter should be used infrequently. The point of view taken by songs such as "I Will Celebrate"[2] by Rita Baloche not only excludes the worshiping community, but it also grounds worship in the thoughts and actions of the worshiper rather than in the work of Christ. There is some precedent in Scripture for this type of expression (Ps. 42:5)[3], and some hymnody takes the same approach ("Be Still, My Soul"), but the worship planner should be cautious when choosing material of this perspective for use in corporate worship and certainly shouldn't encourage a repertoire of songs that lean in this direction.

Worship Action

The second category deals with worship actions, or as Ron Rienstra calls them, "objective" song categories. Rienstra's point is that while we frequently choose songs for their subjective effect (an upbeat praise set, a slow emotional song), we should be more concerned with what the songs actually communicate. He lists categories such as celebration, adoration, confession/lamentation, redemption, preparation (for proclamation), intercession/supplication, dedication.[4] A broad range of worship actions like this encourages a healthy spiritual diet and also shifts the planner's focus from choosing music that achieves an emotional effect—making a participant *feel* joyful, somber, awe-filled—to building a repertoire that achieves spiritual impact, leading the worshiper into confession, thanksgiving, and dedication. Of course, the two are not mutually exclusive, but the primary goal should be spiritual impact.

In both of the above categories, we can use the Psalms as a rubric against which we measure our own worship repertoire. The Psalms are God-focused, but they don't exclude the human condition. They encourage communal expression but don't exclude the first person. They are full of praise but also full of lament and supplication. Many worship planners focus only on upbeat songs of praise, but the Psalms aren't like that and neither is life.

Liturgical Function

This category analyzes how a song functions within the church year and the weekly worship format. Every church should have songs for use during church seasons such as Easter, Advent, and Christmas, and for parts of its weekly worship services such as altar calls, creeds, and benedictions. Of course, each church shapes its yearly and weekly worship differently, depending on its theology and tradition. Danger arises when a church begins to change its theology to fit its music, as in the case of worship planners who eliminate corporate confession because they have adopted a "celebration" song repertoire, or a church that has all "come to Jesus" songs but no "go out to serve" songs.

Song Subject

Fostering a repertoire with a broad range of subjects is not only important for sermon- and theme-oriented worship services. Singing about the work of the Holy Spirit, Jesus's resurrection, sanctification, and evangelism will help grow Christians who understand and act upon these themes. Listen to Cornelius Plantinga's evaluation of the themes he found (or didn't find) in Word Music's popular collection *Songs for Praise and Worship*:

> Only three songs even mention all three persons of the Holy Trinity, and no songs focus upon the Holy Trinity itself. No songs even mention the Trinity, or the tri-unity, or the three-in-oneness of God. No songs do that. Not even one song. Very few Praise and Worship

songs praise God for the church, either, or for covenant or for holy communion, and none do this for baptism, the sacrament that publicly recognizes our union with Christ and with the body of Christ.[5]

Is it any wonder that few Christians understand concepts such as the Trinity on either a cognitive or intuitive level? Worship leaders have the opportunity to put these themes on their tongues and in their hearts.

Frequency of Use

On a practical level, the frequency with which a song is used describes not only which themes are voiced but how often. For example, churches that use hymnals have over five hundred hymns available to them, spanning every topic imaginable from every era of the Christian church, yet few churches use more than one hundred of those. Typically the songs used are those that reflect the beliefs of the pastor or worship planner; inevitably their constant use will shape the beliefs of the people as well. It is good to keep records of how often songs are used in order to monitor prevalent and recurring worship themes. Keeping lists of songs receiving heavy, medium, and light usage also gives the worship planner data that is useful when determining whether, for example, a particular song is familiar enough to be confidently sung as an opening song.

Music Style

We could argue that the entire history of Christian worship is one of contemporary and vernacular branches being grafted into the larger historic tree—too much tradition and the tree decays, too much contemporary and the tree loses its roots. Analyzing repertoire along these lines clarifies the balance between historic and modern sources. However, these are not the only matters of balance in worship. Paul Westermeyer argues that "the message takes musical shape not in the abstract, but in the actual 'incarnate' ethnic sounds of given peoples," but that there also "must be some way in which we not only sing our individual ethnic songs, but also sing something more universal."[6] Musically, this attempt to balance the individuality of the local church with the universality of the global and historic body of Christ may mean combining songs that are important and unique to your local congregation—perhaps even written by a member—with songs such as "Amazing Grace," "Lord, I Lift Your Name on High," and "Siyahamba," which are used by Christians throughout the world and throughout history.

Of course, categorizing a church's repertoire is not as easy as it appears on paper—many songs have a number of functions within each category, data about frequency of use may not be available, and those assessing the repertoire may disagree about the categories or how each song fits within a category. However, we must do our best to be caretakers of the people's song, knowing that the environment and repeated elements of worship are strong factors in the spiritual growth of worshipers. Gary Burge's insight into a pastor's role in worship also sheds light on the role of music in worship:

> When I come to my kitchen hungry, I often take the food that is most easily within reach. When we come to worship empty, we assimilate those images that are most accessible. . . . As they [pastors] conduct worship, they set patterns in place that form the image of God in worshippers' minds.[7]

Evaluating Song Quality

> Music of the congregation needs to be congregational. . . . Congregations cannot count irregular or lengthy rests from any period or style. They cannot do overly complicated syncopations. They cannot, as a rule, sing augmented fourths or major sevenths or other such leaps that are not carefully prepared. They cannot generally sing what is conceived for a soloist. . . . The worshiping assembly can do what human beings without rehearsal can do—sing simple musical structures in an idiom they understand, structures that make logical musical sense, so that they can be remembered easily enough for singing among normal people.[8]

A musical technician like myself knows perfectly well that this "excellent" music is often quite mediocre—honest and plain stuff, but nothing to write home about. The "typical" parishes should get out of the business of trying to sound excellent all the time; instead, they should concentrate their musical efforts on good, wholesome, plain, homely music.[9]

Both Paul Westermeyer and Thomas Day drive home the point that congregational song must be judged differently than music for orchestras, pop bands, soloists, or hit radio. Congregational song is a functional art in which all other artistic impulses must be submitted to the skills and benefit of the collective voice of the congregation.

General Traits of Quality Congregational Songs

In order to effectively evaluate modern music for worship, we must first evaluate traits that have marked quality congregational songs throughout the history of Christianity—singability, lyric quality, and music scalability.

SINGABILITY

Because congregational song must ultimately be sung by a group of untrained singers, it is important to remain focused on their needs and abilities.

Range and tessitura. One of the primary issues of singability in congregational song is range. The voice of the average untrained singer seems to be lowering over time, perhaps because people today learn the use of the chest voice from modern pop music. Many newer hymnals have dropped the keys of historic hymns to accommodate this change. A comfortable range for a congregation spans from B♭ below middle C to the D a tenth above that, with men and women's ranges replicated one octave apart. Many can temporarily stretch a step or two above or below this range, but others will find this difficult or uncomfortable.

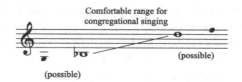

Comfortable range for
congregational singing

(possible)

(possible)

While this describes the overall available range, it doesn't take into account tessitura, or the range in which the bulk of the notes lie. For instance, the chorus of Darlene Zschech's "Shout to the Lord" is not particularly high, but its repetition of the notes around the A causes some vocal fatigue for the average singer. This same song provides the opportunity to see the interaction between range and tessitura: the song dips down to a low G# in the beginning of the verse, eliminating the possibility of transposing the song any lower to ease the fatigue caused by the chorus. This doesn't make the song unusable, but it certainly pushes the limits of what a congregation can sing.

Rhythm. A second major stumbling block for congregational singing is the use of complicated rhythm. This is not to imply that anything more complicated than the even rhythms of hymnody are unusable. On the contrary, there is always an interplay between rhythm, melody, and harmony in congregational song; an increase of complexity in one area will usually necessitate less complexity in another. Hymnody is generally rich in harmonic interest but rhythmically simple.

Syncopation, pattern, and tempo are the three factors that affect rhythmic complexity. One of the reasons syncopation can create difficulties for group singing is that there are numerous ways to syncopate any given rhythm. The plethora of interpretive possibilities introduces instability into the congregation's singing, whose goal in worship is musical unity. Of course, the ability of different groups to sing syncopation will vary greatly. It is important to discern what is appropriate for each group of worshipers, embracing lively rhythms as a valid and exciting aspect of worship music, but not frustrating and alienating the people with rhythms that are too difficult to sing with unity.

Rhythmic complexity can be somewhat mitigated by the judicious use of repeated patterns. These patterns, or rhythmic motives, help unite a song artistically and give singers the regularity and repetition needed to aid memory. The song must achieve balance between originality and unpredictability on the one hand, and motivic monotony on the other. For example, Andraé Crouch uses the same quarter, quarter, quarter, eighth, eighth rhythm throughout "Soon and Very

Soon," which gives a regular pattern for the singer to follow; yet he provides relief from that motive at the "Hallelujah!" which saves the song from rhythmic tedium. On a smaller scale, Michael W. Smith ties together the first phrase of "How Majestic Is Your Name" by using the same rhythm on the words "O Lord, our Lord" and "Your name in all." On the other end of the spectrum is the verse of Joel Houston's "Everyday" which has no predictable pattern; it is a great pop song but is not conducive to group singing.

Form. The final consideration in the singability of music intended for a congregation is form. Because the majority of the people in the pews cannot read music, the songs they sing must be simple enough to learn and remember without the use of music. It is no accident that music from the oral tradition has tended toward simple musical forms such as call-and-response (musical themes volleyed between the leader and the congregation), strophic (multiple verses of text with the same music), and verse-chorus forms. These structures are short and repetitious, allowing the least sophisticated musical minds to comprehend them quickly. A question of form rises when considering the recent trend in Praise & Worship toward including a "bridge." The bridge in pop music is a short, non-repeated section intended to contrast the verse and chorus; however, this is of questionable value in congregational song because it increases the complexity of the song's form.

Lyric Quality

Solid theology. When analyzing the theology of a text, remember that every song should express *some* aspect of truth, but no single song can express *all* truth. Revealing the whole theology is the role of repertoire; each individual song is one piece of that unfolding revelation. Therefore, the most important consideration is that no individual song has incorrect theology—falsehood will never serve to build a repertoire that shows a true picture of God. Texts of no substance should be avoided, because they add nothing to the overall truth of the church's repertoire. In the same way that a decision to drink a diet soda is also a decision *not* to drink something beneficial like water, milk, or juice, songs of no substance are chosen at the expense of those that will contribute to the health of the worshiper. As John Bertalot laments

666

with tongue firmly in cheek, "So many songs seem to give the message, 'I love buttercups and so does Jesus. Alleluia!'"[10] May our churches be filled with songs that are more substantial than that!

Artistry of expression. Because congregational song is a functional art, "artistry" has different implications for the congregational songwriter than for the poet. The text of a congregational song must balance the need for the whole body to sing in unity and the need for the individual worshiper to be engaged in that collective expression. That may mean writing from the "we" perspective or the collective "I," but never in the first person without regard for the collective voice. The writer must tap into the vein of modern expression while taking care to give timeless truth the dignity it deserves. Overly colloquial language trivializes the message and guarantees the brevity of the text's life. One only needs to flip through some of the songbooks produced during the Jesus movement to see examples of this. What once seemed so "groovy" is now hopelessly dated. (Is it any wonder that we no longer sing "Hallelujah, Outasight!"; "Heaven's Gonna Be a Blast!"; or the anachronistic "In Tune with Thee"?) Finally, the text should be lyrical rather than poetic—lyrics are intended for singing, whereas poetry is meant for reading. Therefore the songwriter will choose words that flow off the tongue easily, perhaps using simpler vocabulary, rather than gravitating toward the dense language and intricate phrases that a slow reading can unpack.

Isaac Watts, by all accounts a successful hymn writer, summarizes well the guidelines for writing quality congregational song texts in this analysis of his own work: "I make no pretenses to the name of poet or polite writer. . . . I am ambitious to be a servant to the churches and a helper to the joy of the meanest [humblest] Christian. . . . I would neither indulge any bold metaphors, nor admit of hard words, nor tempt the ignorant worshipper to sing without his understanding."[11]

MUSIC SCALABILITY

The musical abilities of worshipers vary widely. Songs should provide a simple point of entry that is accessible to all and at the same time include more sophisticated musical elements that will retain the interest of the musically advanced. There is a beautiful example of this type of scalability in the music of the BaAka of central Africa. The BaAka value individual expression within the fabric of community, so their singing builds layers of melody that each singer can alter slightly according to taste (heterophony); once the whole community is singing, individuals are welcome to improvise lines that enhance the group's sound in unique ways.[12] There are examples of this balance of individual and communal expressions within congregational music as well. Harmonies provide an opportunity for music readers to add multiple layers to hymns while less advanced singers can continue to sing the melody. Echoes and descants serve a similar purpose, as do the improvised harmonies that are common in folk and pop. The important thing is that the melody can be sung immediately by children and non-musicians, and that the song is flexible enough to allow for increased musical contributions with repeated use.

Differences between Hymnody and Praise & Worship

Before moving from the universal traits of congregational song quality to an evaluation of quality in the Praise & Worship genre, we must discuss the differences between hymnody and Praise & Worship. The two are often compared to each other, resulting in criticisms of Praise & Worship songs based on the values of hymns, or vice versa. Both are unique forms and should be evaluated on their own merits. For the sake of brevity, hymns will be defined here as all historic congregational songs still in common use.

DEVELOPMENT VERSUS REPETITION

Hymns typically develop one idea, whereas Praise & Worship songs repeat an idea. "When I Survey the Wondrous Cross" is a wonderful example of thematic development in hymns. Watts starts with an image of Christ on the cross and leads the singer deeper into his suffering with each subsequent verse, until the final verse forces the worshiper to conclude that dedication to Jesus is the only logical response: "Were the whole realm of nature mine, that were a present far too small. Love so amazing, so divine, demands my soul, my life, my all." The rhetorical development is convincing, and when wedded to music, it exacts a powerful emotional response as well.

Praise & Worship songs tend to take a single idea and repeat it verbatim or with slight variations. For example, Rick Founds's "Lord, I Lift Your Name on High" has some lyrical development within the structure of the song (heaven; earth; cross; grave; sky), but when that structure is finished, it simply repeats. Other songs feature slight variations, such as "Glorify Thy Name" by Donna Adkins; it begins with "Father, we love You" and then substitutes "Jesus, we love You" and "Spirit, we love You" in subsequent repetitions. This is variation rather than development.

Even the Praise & Worship songs that do have multiple verses with completely different texts tend to use the verses to expand the scope of the theme before arriving again at the chorus rather than as development or refinement of the theme. The closest that Praise & Worship comes to hymnlike development is in some of the works of Graham Kendrick ("Meekness and Majesty") and Keith Getty ("In Christ Alone").

Exegetical versus Meditational

In the use of Scripture, hymns tend to be exegetical and Praise & Worship songs more meditational. That is, hymns tend to utilize a whole passage of Scripture or exegete a larger scriptural idea. Praise & Worship songs, once again, utilize repetition. Often a short passage will be repeated in a meditative way, such as Michael Ledner's "You Are My Hiding Place." When multiple verses are used, they rarely include another section of the same passage; instead, they may use other similar Scripture passages such as the three verses of Jesus's teachings in Karen Lafferty's "Seek Ye First," or they may go in an entirely different, and perhaps non-scriptural, direction, as in "As the Deer" by Martin Nystrom.

Strophic versus Verse/Chorus

The third difference deals with form. Hymns, especially before the advent of gospel songs and frontier hymns, are mainly strophic—that is, multiple verses of text using the same music. Praise & Worship songs are true to their musical roots, using the verse/chorus structure common to pop and folk music, and increasingly adding the bridge found in pop.

Four-Part versus Unison with Accompaniment

Hymns, regardless of their origin, are most often published in four-part settings intended for congregational singing with piano or organ accompaniment. This density of harmony has led to a predominance of simple rhythms, mainly quarter and half notes.[13] In contrast, praise songs tend to use highly rhythmic and syncopated unison melodies accompanied by the rhythm section of the standard pop band. This separation of melody and rhythmic accompaniment is in many ways optimal, because it allows the accompaniment to become complex and creative while the congregation sings a simple melody—a format seen in folk music throughout the world.

Independent versus Medleys

Finally, hymns can stand by themselves as an independent musical unit more easily than Praise & Worship songs. Because hymns develop more fully and have their harmonies encapsulated within their structures, there is a strong sense of conclusion at the close of a hymn. In Praise & Worship songs, on the other hand, the form itself doesn't convey strong cues for closure—should it be repeated two times or three times?—so they are less satisfying when sung independently. For this reason Praise & Worship songs tend to be performed in medleys where each song flows into the next, creating longer and more satisfying musical units, and allowing the texts to embellish and develop each other.

All these differences are quantitative rather than qualitative: just because a hymn fulfills one function better than a Praise & Worship song doesn't invalidate Praise & Worship, and vice versa. It would behoove critics to be more broad-minded and kindhearted in their analyses. For instance, a hymn purist who decries the simplicity and repetition of Praise & Worship would be obliged to also decry the same traits in Taizé and much global hymnody as well. Critics of hymnody may find it hard to muster any enthusiasm for the more austere rhythms of hymns, yet they certainly sing Christmas carols with gusto! We must be open to different styles of worship music without feeling the need to endorse everything within the style. Instead, seek out the best of each genre and place it in the worship service where it functions effectively.

Perhaps this old joke best illustrates the point of praise songs and hymns being "just different":

A farmer was in the city on business one weekend. While he was there, he attended one of the city's churches. Upon returning home, his wife asked him what it was like at the city church.

"Oh, it was a lot like our country church, except they sang these things called 'praise choruses' instead of hymns."

"Praise choruses? What are those?" asked the wife.

"Well, they're sort of like hymns, just different."

"Different how?"

"Well . . . it's sort of like this. If I said, 'Martha, the cows are in the corn,' it would be a hymn.

"Now if I said, 'Martha, Martha, Martha, the cows, the white cows, the brown cows, the black cows, the cows, the cows, the cows, are in the corn, in the corn, the corn. Oh, Martha, the cows are in the corn,' that would be a praise chorus!"

Or the sequel about hymns:

It just so happened that the same weekend, a businessman was in the country and went to a country church. Upon returning home, his wife asked him how the service was.

"Pretty much the same as ours, except we sang hymns instead of praise choruses."

"Hymns?" his wife replied. "I think my mother told me about those! What were they like?"

"Oh, sort of like a praise chorus except different."

"And that difference would be?"

"All right, if I were to say, 'Mary, the cows are in the corn,' that would be a praise chorus.

"On the other hand, if I said, 'O Mary, wife of my youth with whom I shall all of my days abide, Incline thine ear and hearken unto my cry! For the cows of varying shades and hues—who can explain their ways? Have left the fields in which they graze and have traversed yonder into the fields of golden corn that gleam in the sun.' THAT would be a hymn!"[14]

Evaluating Praise & Worship Songs

The same general traits that are found in quality congregational songs throughout the ages will also be found in modern worship songs, but in many cases the specific applications will be different. Here we will uncover these unique characteristics of the Praise & Worship genre and study examples of both lyrics and music in order to establish a process for further song evaluation in the genre.

Lyrics

Conversational language. Many of the same text evaluation principles discussed previously will apply here, but because the Praise & Worship genre draws from the vernacular, there is a noticeable relaxation of poetic style. The songs use simple, everyday words in a conversational manner. Though some songs lapse into colloquial chumminess, there is much to be gained from this loose, familiar use of language: it emphasizes the friendship we have with our Lord (John 15:14–15) and his incarnational desire to be involved in our everyday lives.

Praise & Worship's emphasis on God's immanence provides a good opportunity to supplement a church's existing repertoire. Additionally, a song's focus on one, bite-size truth provides an opportunity for the worshiper to do the same. This meditative quality is accompanied by a more subjective lyrical perspective. This combination can very powerfully allow a truth to become a first-person prayer or affirmation that works its way deep into the soul.

Colloquialism. Praise & Worship is not the only genre to run the risk of being overly colloquial, but it is frequently criticized in this area, and not without reason. For example, the seldom-used verses of Rich Mullins's "Our God Is an Awesome God" contain phrases such as "When He rolls up His sleeves He ain't just putting on the ritz." This is ill-suited to the majesty of the chorus and certainly lacks the dignity that one would hope to see when the Lord of the universe is being described. Another poetic *faux pas* arises in Graham Kendrick's "Knowing You." Overall, the song is a wonderful recasting of Philippians 3:7–11 until the chorus: "Knowing You, Jesus, knowing You, there is no greater thing. You're my all, You're the best, You're my joy, my righteousness, and I love You, Lord." One can almost picture the writer giving Jesus a playful punch on the shoulder and exclaiming, "Jesus, you're the best."

Inappropriate imagery. Sometimes a songwriter's choice of words exhibits not only a lack of poetic finesse but questionable theology. In 2002 a song promoted nationally to worship leaders included the lyric (sung to the Lord), "I just can't make it one more night without Your kiss." This kind of imagery, coupled with the music of a sensuous love song, reduces Jesus to the level of the run-of-the-mill infatuation who exists to fulfill us in the way we feel we want to be fulfilled. It has nothing to do with the life-giving love of Jesus who calls us to follow him in the way of the cross. If we hope that our worship will help shape the people of the congregation into Christ-likeness, we must be careful to choose songs that are strongly biblical rather than romantic, trivial, or therapeutic.

Church editorial policy. We should also be aware of any church editorial policies that would affect our song choices. For instance, churches may discourage the use of the first-person perspective, disallow non-inclusive language, or disfavor songs that utilize King James English. This may necessitate changing "Brethren, We Have Met to Worship" to "Christians, We Have Met to Worship" or "I Exalt Thee" to "We Exalt You." An interesting example of this kind of policy is the change made to Twila Paris's "He Is Exalted" in the ELCA's *Worship and Praise Songbook*. Because the original lyrics never actually state *who* is being exalted, the editors changed the chorus from "He is the Lord" to "Jesus is Lord." A useful guideline is to make these changes judiciously and without stirring controversy among those in the congregation who love the song. If the song must be mangled to adhere to a particular editorial policy, then it is best to simply find a different song.

The above principles for evaluating texts may seem overly cerebral and detailed, so perhaps a simple rule of thumb will suffice: never choose songs with passable lyrics—choose songs with lyrics that will change people's lives. As John Witvliet remarks: "Most congregations really know only 200 songs or hymns. . . . Suppose there are 20,000 songs available. You are then identifying the top 1% of extant resources. We have the luxury of being very, very picky."[15]

Music

Just as the lyrics of the Praise & Worship genre diverge from historic congregational song due in part to their vernacular origins, the music of the genre has more similarities to modern styles of secular music than it does to anything in the church's worship tradition.

Hook. The essence of the pop song is the "hook," a trait shared by Praise & Worship songs. A hook is a unique melodic line, chord sequence, or rhythm that instantly identifies it from any other song. Broadway's ascending tritone of "Maria" (Leonard Bernstein), rock's unforgettable opening guitar riff in "Smoke on the Water" (Deep Purple), and big band's shouted "Pennsylvania 6-5000" (Glenn Miller) are all hooks that have embedded themselves into our collective musical memory. In the same way, the opening bass tenths of Darrell Evans's "Trading My Sorrows" and the *do-ti-sol* melodic line of Twila Paris's "He Is Exalted" are the fingerprints that distinguish these songs.

Thematic coherence. The hook provides the musical seed from which the rest of the song grows. This thematic coherence is especially important in pop music because the musical forms are so compact. Most songs have a verse and a chorus, and some have a short transition between the two called a "pre-chorus" or a brief thematic sidestep called a "bridge." With so few structural options, it is important that each song has not only an internal coherence growing from the hook but also enough contrasting material to avoid tedium. This can be seen in "He Is Exalted." The song is more or less in an AABA form with the first A introducing the melodic hook mentioned above and the second A extending the phrase and rising to the B theme. The B theme contrasts the eighth-note movement of the A section with a legato dotted-quarter-note theme. The return to the final A theme is refreshing not only because it is a recapitulation of previous material but also because it is at a higher pitch level and set to new chords. This provides a good example of the unity and variety that makes for a coherent praise song.

Of course, lyrical or musical evaluation doesn't *determine* quality; it simply provides some reasons for an initial aesthetic reaction. A repertoire based solely on personal taste is never adequate, but it is wise to listen carefully to your own intuitive evaluation. Is the song memorable and interesting? When the novelty of the song wears off, is it of high enough quality to sustain interest? Is the popularity of the song tainting an honest evaluation of it? Is stylistic difference an excuse for accepting mediocre quality (or rejecting high quality)?

In the final analysis, the head and heart must come together in a prayerful attitude to discern which songs are appropriate for a particular situation. These will be songs that express the worshipers' hearts and shape their thoughts with what is true, noble, right, pure, lovely, admirable, excellent, and praiseworthy (see Phil. 4:8).

Finding New Praise Songs

Jesus told them another parable: "The kingdom of heaven is like a man who sowed good seed in his field. But while everyone was sleeping, his enemy came and sowed weeds among the wheat, and went away. When the wheat sprouted and formed heads, then the weeds also appeared.

"The owner's servants came to him and said, 'Sir, didn't you sow good seed in your field? Where then did the weeds come from?'

"'An enemy did this,' he replied.

"The servants asked him, 'Do you want us to go and pull them up?'

"'No,' he answered, 'because while you are pulling the weeds, you may root up the wheat with them. Let both grow together until the harvest. At that time I will tell the harvesters: First collect the weeds and tie them in bundles to be burned; then gather the wheat and bring it into my barn.'"

Matthew 13:24–30

Presumably, Christ's parable of the wheat and weeds wasn't told with music in mind, but it does remind us of a basic principle of musical longevity: worship renewals grow new worship music, some of which will be harvested for use by following generations, much of which will wither away in the next season of renewal. This constant sifting of the church's song means that only songs of transcendent excellence remain from the early history of the church while much of questionable long-term value is currently being produced. Critics of Praise & Worship have used the existence of weeds to dismiss the genre as a whole, but this seems shortsighted. After all, the fact that Isaac Watts wrote hymns such as "Blest Is the Man Whose Bowels Move" doesn't negate his permanent contributions to the church's worship!

The modern music minister's task is to be part of the winnowing process, seeking high-quality songs that are appropriate to his or her local context and that may also be left for future generations. But where does one turn for resources in this endeavor?

Worship Community

Delegation is a vital principle to any successful leader, and worship leadership is no exception. Rather than shouldering the burden of finding quality praise songs oneself, the worship leader should seek the input of colleagues, groups within one's church, and worship volunteers. This not only eases the worship leader's workload, but it also fosters ownership among ministry partners.

Colleagues. Immediate colleagues such as other staff members are valuable because they understand the worship leader's particular church context; however, they are also less likely to be able to recommend fresh song suggestions outside of the church's current repertoire. Colleagues and friends from other churches, whether distant or local, are another good source for song suggestions. These are the people who will take the time for a conversation about new developments in their church's worship, and who will also have a different perspective, taste, and context that will broaden one's own experience.

Conferences, workshops, and visiting other churches. Worship conferences inevitably have a time of group worship in which the worship leader is chosen in part for a unique musical style, good reputation, and particular song repertoire. These events are likely to introduce some exciting new songs, so keeping bulletins and notes is important. Attending workshops about particular songwriters or music styles is another excellent way to open doors into new repertoire. Finally, attending worship services while on vacation is a way to observe songs in an authentic, week-to-week context that the "best behavior" atmosphere of conferences and workshops can't provide. Remember that worship leaders are usually glad to share their repertoire suggestion; if a song or service is particularly compelling, it will be fruitful to approach the leader for more information.

Magazines, books, email lists, and websites. While there are many magazines that provide reviews of choral octavos, there are few that review individual congregational songs. However, artist highlights, songbook and CD reviews, and even advertisements offer information about what is available in modern worship. Some books[16] provide song lists as part of their larger discussion. If the reader feels an affinity with the views of the author, he or she will probably also like the suggested songs. Email lists are a good place to discuss repertoire; requests for "Christmas songs for worship team" or "congregational songs for baptism" are often met with a flurry of responses. Finally, church and independent worship websites often provide lists of songs, giving a glimpse into the active repertoire of other churches.[17]

Small groups. Bible studies, cell groups, college fellowships, youth groups, marriage or renewal retreats, and Christian education classes are often eager to recommend songs that have been meaningful in their own worship times. Because these groups often represent the most vibrant corners of a church's spiritual life, the songs can be an indigenous expression of what the Holy Spirit is doing in the church. Capitalizing on an existing work of the Spirit and the accompanying enthusiasm is wiser than trying to manufacture something new.

There are many ways that the streams of worship from small groups can flow into the river of the larger church's worship. Perhaps a song has emerged from a retreat or summer camp that summarizes the mountaintop experience of those involved. Having the participants teach the song to the congregation is a way of highlighting the event and its spiritual importance, validating the experience to the larger congregation, and spreading the message or theme of the retreat in song. Likewise, churches that have annual youth or university Sundays should treat these worship services not as "show and tell" but as a time to build bridges and grow community through a shared worship experience. The music minister should work closely with the youth or university fellowship in order to ensure the use of elements that will be familiar to the larger church body as well as the introduction of new materials that will be usable in future worship services. In fact, it is helpful to solidify the music that has been introduced by using it again the following week.

Worship volunteers. Those who comprise the worship team and other worship ensembles are involved in the worship life of the church because they care about worship. They bring a myriad of worship histories and interests to the church, which provide depth and breadth to the community. The music minister who encourages song suggestions from worship volunteers will have a steady stream of music coming from volunteers' former churches, friends (and friends of friends), and perhaps even some penned by the volunteers themselves. It is important to value volunteer input while retaining the right to make the final decision about a song. This can be handled effectively by thanking the volunteer for the suggestion, seriously considering the song, and following up by explaining why the song will or will not be used.

Worship Industry

While the worship community can make impartial song recommendations, the worship industry makes them available in the form of printed music, recordings, and Internet resources.

Maranatha! There are many publishers in the Praise & Worship genre, but the market has thus far rested on three seasoned companies. Maranatha! Music, founded in 1972, is the company most closely associated with the Jesus movement of the late 60s and early 70s—which is the source of the Praise & Worship genre. From their roots in Chuck Smith's Calvary Chapel in Costa Mesa, California, they have gone on to produce the ever-popular *Praise Chorus Book*, successful recordings such as the twenty-volume Praise series, live worship events such as Promise Keepers, and training events such as the Worship Leader Workshop; they have even teamed up with Zondervan to publish the *NIV Worship Bible.*

Integrity. In 1987, Integrity Media was created to help "people worldwide experience the manifest presence of God."[18] Today it claims 64 percent of the worship market with a line of products that includes the Vertical Music and Urban Praise labels, Seminars 4 Worship, and the Time-Life blockbuster *Songs 4 Worship*, which is the best-selling worship CD of all time.

Vineyard. Vineyard Music Group is a nonprofit organization founded in 1982 by John Wimber. Though they remain committed to publishing worship resources from and for Vineyard churches, the company has had a substantial impact on modern worship in the larger church. Vineyard's post-Pentecostal philosophy of intimate, vertically focused worship takes the form of the guitar-driven folk rock of the Touching the Father's Heart series as well as the newer sounds of their Y-Worship series. Interestingly, Maranatha!, Integrity, and Vineyard have recently joined forces to produce the extremely successful WOW Worship series of CDs and songbooks.

Worship Explosion. While Maranatha!, Integrity, and Vineyard represent the ongoing legacy of the Jesus movement, there has recently been another wave of worship renewal often dubbed the "worship explosion." Worship leaders such as Australian Darlene Zschech ("Shout to the Lord") and Englishmen Martin Smith (of the band Delirious) and Matt Redman ("The Heart of Worship") write songs that capture the imaginations of a new generation of worshipers. Whereas the older modern worship music tended to be more compatible with the consumeristic, passive, and hierarchal approach to worship that had been espoused in seeker and celebration worship models, the music of the worship explosion tends to be a less polished, more participatory grassroots movement. New record labels such as Worship Together, Sixsteprecords, and Here to Him were formed to bring the new sound to market. Maranatha!, Integrity, and Vineyard are also beginning to ride this worship wave by creating new labels and series directed toward this youth-driven market segment. While this new style brings a refreshing authenticity to worship, it is not without its flaws: this goateed, postmodern crowd seems suspicious of anyone over twenty and views songs that have been sung for more than a few years as outdated.[19]

Internet. As is true of every medium today, the Internet has provided a place for hundreds of independent publishers and self-publishers to make their wares available. These range from information sites run by established songwriters and performers such as Paul Baloche to homegrown sites such as www.songsofpraise.org. The quality varies tremendously, but gems can be found. Many songs are offered for free. To find websites of more established artists, search under the person's name. For online song collections try www.sharesong.org or www .freepraiseandworship.org, or peruse the site lists at Yahoo! (http:// dir.yahoo.com/Entertainment/Music/Genres/Religious_and_De votional/Christian/Worship) or About.com (http://christianmusic .about.com).

The important thing to remember about specific publishers is that they are in business to make money. Though they may have honorable intentions, their primary goal is to sell a product, not provide what is healthy or appropriate for the local congregation. Having said that, a buyer who has a healthy suspicion of the industry can find fine music for sale and will soon discover publishers whose style fits his or her local worship context.

Song Services

Another source of new songs coming from the worship industry is song introduction or rating services. These Top 40 style resources and publications are the best way to stay abreast of the "latest and greatest" Praise & Worship songs.

CCLI. The longest-running service of this type is Christian Copyright Licensing International. CCLI is primarily a royalty collection agency, but it also provides a list of the top twenty-five songs for the latest six-month reporting period (http://www.ccli .com/WorshipResources/Top25.cfm). Even if these songs are not part of a church's repertoire, every modern worship leader should learn all of the songs, because they are statistically the most univer- sally used and recognized in the Praise & Worship repertoire.

Song DISCovery. While CCLI's list shows the most popular praise songs that are actually being used in congregations around the world, Song DISCovery introduces the songs that are currently being promoted by the worship industry. An affiliate of *Worship Leader* magazine, Song DISCovery is a bimonthly CD and leadsheet song collection that is sent to twenty thousand subscribers. Each volume showcases ten to twelve new songs, largely songs by major labels. Though the tracks often do more to showcase the artist than the song, the service is the best way to monitor trends in the industry.

Song Collections

Presifted song collections are similar to hymnals in that they seek to gather the best quality that the industry has to offer. Because assessing quality requires the perspective that only time can give, most of these song collections feature older material (i.e., five to thirty years old).

WOW Worship. The freshest of the presifted resources are found in the *WOW Worship* series, which is essentially a "greatest hits" compilation of the previous three years, released in both CD and piano/vocal score. While the collection is valuable for its song choices, the piano parts are typically too difficult for the average church pianist.

The Source. Edited by veteran worship leader and songwriter Graham Kendrick and published by Kevin Mayhew, *The Source* (volumes 1 and 2) is a huge hardcover collection of songs with a definite slant toward British songwriters.

The Best of the Best. Not quite as mainstream but worthy of mention is *The Best of the Best: The Other Songbook 2*, released by Fellowship Publications. It features a well-chosen selection of modern worship music, the most helpful indices of any modern songbook, and a well-written piano accompaniment edition.

Renew! Robert Webber has produced an excellent hymnal, *Renew!*, which is especially appropriate for "convergence" churches. Because of its liturgical bent, it draws on a good deal of material from GIA, Hope, OCP, and other publishers outside the typical Praise & Worship fare.

The Celebration Hymnal. Touted as "the hymnal for blended worship," *The Celebration Hymnal* is a joint publication by Word and

Integrity that compiles the most popular songs of both hymnody and Praise & Worship. It is a good choice for blended churches needing a hymnal, but the contemporary repertoire leans very heavily toward Integrity copyrights.

The Praise and Worship Fake Book. If you don't need piano parts, Brentwood-Benson's collection is a great choice. It contains over five hundred songs in leadsheet format—melody, lyrics, and chords.

Denominational Resources

Even the denominations with the richest worship heritages are realizing that modern worship expressions are here to stay. Therefore, they are publishing their own hymnal supplements and modern resources in order to promote new music that is compatible with the denomination's theology. These resources are especially helpful for those who want a denominational or theological "stamp of approval," those who are seeking heavier lyrical content or music for specific liturgical acts, and those who would like to be introduced to denominational composers who may not be known in wider Praise & Worship circles. A number of these resources are worthy of mention.

Worship and Praise. The Lutheran (ELCA) *Worship and Praise* was one of the earliest denominational supplements to include Praise & Worship, and it is also one of the best. It includes careful selections from popular Praise & Worship repertoire combined with Lutheran composers such as Handt Hanson. One can see the mark of Martin Luther in the singability and richness of theology.

Sing! A New Creation. In the same way, the mark of John Calvin is felt in the CRC/RCA project, *Sing! A New Creation.* Included is an ample selection of psalms as well as solid offerings from the global church and modern hymnody. Additionally, the worship leader's edition contains piano parts, performance suggestions, biblical references and background for each song, as well as excellent essays about each style represented in the book.

The Faith We Sing. Another collection that includes a broad selection of modern hymnody as well as Praise & Worship is *The Faith We Sing* from the United Methodist Church.

Other Worship Traditions

Some evangelicals give the impression that they invented worship during the Jesus movement—nothing could be further from the truth! Christians have been worshiping since the time of Christ in every part of the world in styles ranging from stoic to ecstatic. Being connected to the church universal is important. One way to achieve this is to join in the myriad of musical expressions that come from non-evangelical or non-Western Christian churches.

Roman Catholic. The Catholic Church went through a major worship renewal even before the Jesus movement began. *The Constitution on Sacred Liturgy,* which issued from Vatican II, encouraged the use of native languages (rather than Latin), instruments, and compositions in modern styles. From this poured forth a flood of new worship materials that has continued unabated to the present. Publishers such as GIA, OCP, and others rival the output of the Praise & Worship industry, releasing new music by Marty Haugen, David Haas, Dan Schutte, and other composers. Some of these songs, such as "Here I Am, Lord" by Dan Schutte, have already been grafted into the Praise & Worship repertoire. Evangelicals would benefit from incorporating Roman Catholic worship music into their repertoire because the Roman Catholic repertoire's attention to biblical text (especially the Psalms), themes of social justice, and a tendency toward melodic singability are often lacking in Praise & Worship.

Taizé. Taizé, an ecumenical community in Southern France, began in 1940 as a place of reconciliation in war-torn Europe. Today the brothers of Taizé receive as many as five thousand visitors per week, many of whom are drawn to the meditative, repetitive songs that are used during daily prayer services. These quiet musical reflections are a welcome antidote to our increasingly busy, noisy world—and sometimes worship services![20]

Iona. The Iona community, based in a restored monastery off the west coast of Scotland, is known for its rustic, Celtic-influenced folk style. The songs, many written by John Bell, frequently address social issues, grief, and other prevalent biblical themes that many churches overlook.[21]

African-American. African-American music has had consider-able influence on American pop music in general, and black gospel is thought to be one of the original sources of the Praise & Wor-ship genre. Most white evangelical churches wouldn't be able to authentically replicate African-American styles, such as the mass choir sound or the hip-hop influence found in the music of Kirk Franklin and others, but there are many songs from spirituals to Thomas Dorsey that are easily transplanted into new worship set-tings. There are also a growing number of churches and perform-ers that blend pop and gospel in an accessible style, most notably Israel and New Breed, Covenant Church of Pittsburgh, and Darlene Zschech (though she is not African-American, her style is highly influenced by black gospel).

Global worship.[22] Interestingly, what the West once considered the mission field has become a mature voice in the Christian church and is now contributing vibrant new worship expressions to the Western church. These songs have a unique perspective, because they come from entirely different cultures with different values—often closer to those of Jesus's culture—and from Christians who have known suffering. Further, they often come from cultures that cherish community and fellowship, offering a refreshing alternative to the individualism of the West. As C. Michael Hawn elaborates:

> Music from other cultural contexts has the potential to express Chris-tian experience in new ways, causing us to reflect upon our worship with a new sense of awareness. The use of international music in our worship has the potential to free us from a culturally-bound religious experience and broaden our spiritual awareness. Consider the exciting possibility of living not just within the culture that currently shapes our symbols of faith, but beyond our culture as Christians. Living beyond our culture calls us to be open to a revelation from God that supersedes the limits of our parochial awareness. The intentional cultivation of international hymnody in the life of a congregation over a period of time can help the participants become aware of God's broader vision for the world through the eyes of Christians whose world view vastly differs from a traditional, white American perspective.[23]

Introducing New Music

In his fascinating book *The Tipping Point*,[24] Malcolm Gladwell likens ideas to infections. He says they are spread by agents called connectors, mavens, and salesmen until they become an epidemic of thought, style, or culture. This same idea can be applied to the church, where change is more often effected by grassroots movements within the church than it is by the church hierarchy. An important technique for the music minister seeking to introduce new music is to identify what Gladwell calls "influencers" within the church and use them as a way to infect the rest of the congregation.

Small groups. Sometimes the most vibrant worship is not taking place in a church's Sunday worship but in smaller, more intense settings like small groups, men's and women's ministries, marriage retreats, college fellowships, and youth groups. Previously, I discussed how these groups can be a source for finding new music, but they can also be excellent ways to introduce a new song to the congregation "through the back door." For example, if all of a church's Bible studies use a particular song as their theme for a season, a large group of church members will know the song and will have a very strong spiritual connection with it. This will make it extremely easy to teach to the larger congregation in the Sunday worship setting.

Children. Marty Haugen calls children "the secret weapon"[25] because adults will do things for children that they will never do for the worship leader. The innocent, infectious quality of the children will make the congregation loosen up and try a new song, a different language, clapping, or sign language. Using children to lead and teach songs also benefits the children—rather than simply being a cute presentation, they are playing an important role in the worship life of the church.

Music readers. The last group of influencers are the music readers of the church who are sitting in the pews every Sunday. This group can have a very positive effect on the overall singing of the congregation. It is wise to provide music for new songs so that the music readers can support the rest of the congregation as they learn a new melody.

Introducing New Songs

Studies have shown that the main factor in musical taste is familiarity. People like what they know. The pop music business operates on this principle, and we have all experienced hearing a song on the radio that sounds oddly familiar and brings up memories and feelings that one can't quite place. Some promoter has worked hard to place that song in a movie precisely because it will feel like an old friend the next time one hears it. This same principle—familiarity equals enjoyment—can be applied to teaching a congregation new songs.

Prepare new songs. In the weeks preceding a congregational song's introduction, an anthem, prelude, or instrumental rendition of the song may be used to acclimate the people to the music. When the worshipers are invited in a following service to sing the song themselves, the experience is more likely to be successful.

Hold a preservice "practice." Many music ministers find it effective to take time before the service to sing through new songs with those who are present in the congregation, perhaps pointing out any melodic difficulties, explaining confusing repeats, or even teaching harmonies. Then, when the song is encountered during the worship service, the congregation can take part immediately, freeing themselves to worship and freeing the worship leader from having to break the flow of the service with explanations.

Play a full introduction. A further possibility for informing the congregation's ear before asking them to sing is to play the full form of the song as an introduction rather than the typical four or eight measures. This can even be combined with a Scripture reading that ties into the theme of the song to further heighten the spiritual impact of the song.

Introduce a song in sections. A final way of introducing a new song to the congregation during worship is to invite them to sing only portions of the song rather than the whole. A sequence such as the following would be one way of letting them hear before singing:

- worship team sings verse 1, chorus, and verse 2
- congregation joins on chorus

- worship team sings verse 3
- congregation joins on chorus, verse 4, and final chorus

Build Repertoire over Time

The point of preparing people for change and introducing new music is not to put the congregation on an endless merry-go-round of novelty but to build a core worship repertoire over time while retaining an atmosphere that allows for ongoing renewal of the repertoire.

Song of the month. A song-of-the-month program is an effective way to slowly add new songs or highlight old ones. It ensures that the congregation will learn twelve songs per year, and when incorporated with song stories printed in the bulletins, choral anthems, testimonies, or interesting variations of text or music, it becomes an educational tool that increases awareness and enthusiasm for congregational singing.

Seasonal songs. Similarly, the use of seasonal or thematic songs can be effective not only for introducing songs but also for teaching about the liturgical year or theology. For example, one song might be used repeatedly during the whole season of Advent, or a song might be sung as preparation for the sermon throughout an entire preaching series.

New-song night. Holding periodic new-song nights is another way of introducing songs. Given the informal, more sparsely attended nature of evening sings, new-song nights also gauge congregational response to songs before introducing them to the whole congregation.

Distribution of recordings. Tapes or CDs of new (or old) repertoire can be distributed to interested church members. Recordings of new songs will increase the number of people who will be able to sing along when the song is introduced during worship, and recordings of old songs will help new members learn the church's repertoire more quickly. Of course, permission must be obtained from the copyright holders.

A concluding admonition for teaching songs is that new or adventurous songs should be introduced at the highest musical level possible. This will minimize distractions and keep the new styles above reproach. To this end the singers should be encouraged to memorize the song.

Solidify the Church's Repertoire

Over time, a church should build a body of songs that is familiar, yet challenging; universal, yet local; broad, yet deep; one that expresses who the people are before God today, yet changes over time as the Spirit works new things in the congregation. The most effective way to solidify the congregation's repertoire is to create a church song collection. This doesn't necessarily mean a physical songbook, but in the same way that a pew hymnal focuses a church's repertoire, this book will narrow the church's repertoire to a manageable, yet meaningful size. Of course, different groups will need different versions of the same collection of songs—congregation, worship team, and director.

Congregation. The congregation's collection may take the form of a hymnal supplement or songbook that resides in the pews. However, creating, maintaining, and updating a book like this requires significant energy. The congregation can have just as secure a sense of repertoire if the songs in the collection are projected on a screen or printed in a bulletin. More important than the format is the emergence of a shared repertoire that represents and reinforces the congregation's shared faith. Whoever prepares the songs for projection or printing should keep one set of master files in a cabinet or computer; this eliminates the need for retyping lyrics or re-finding copyright information and allows editorial errors to be slowly weeded from the repertoire.

Worship team. The singers and players need a very different format than the congregation. The whole worship team needs a large format leadsheet (words, melody, and chords), and individual members may need specific parts such as vocal harmonies, piano parts, and descants. All team members should be expected to keep their own books updated and with them at every rehearsal and service; this eliminates the need to make photocopies every week for songs that are already part of the repertoire and decreases the chances that the team will have to relearn music that is already in the book. The most useful format for the worship team's collection is a three-ring binder with songs hole-punched on both sides to allow for two-page layout when necessary.

Director. The director's files should be complete master files of everything—the congregation's version, worship team format, instrumental parts, and alternative arrangements or keys. It is convenient to keep all of these files in a folder arranged alphabetically by title in a file cabinet. Further, it is helpful to mark originals in colored pen (for instance, underlining the song title), so the master never becomes confused with the copies. This allows photocopies to be stored in the folder, saving copy time before future rehearsals. Additionally, creating a database or spreadsheet will allow the worship planner to search by author, theme, key, or Scripture reference, or easily track the number of times the song has been used.

All of these techniques must serve the overall goal: encouraging enthusiastic participation of the congregation in a body of songs that is both stable and constantly evolving. The worship leader sings each song ten or twenty times more during preparation than the congregation does during worship, so the temptation is to move on to new material quickly. This can be a disastrous impulse! Instead, the worship planner should introduce between one song per month and one song per week. When the congregation has two hundred songs in their repertoire, new songs should be added only as old ones are retired.

4

Planning Worship

The Art of Worship

Though worship is considered the first priority of the Christian life, worship *leadership* is treated as if it were the illegitimate offspring of music and religion. Many musicians see it as something that lesser musicians do if they can't make it in "real" music, or something they themselves do if they need some extra cash. Some pastors look down on church musicians who lack seminary training. Because it is viewed as such a rudimentary activity in both musical and religious circles, there are many who question the need for specific training in worship.

Worship is a unique art form combining music, theology, performance, history, Scripture, leadership, technology, architecture, art, and drama. It requires organizational, pastoral, and communication skills outside of the worship service as well. All these disciplines collide in the messy, beautiful world of music ministry. A musician, a pastor, or an artist may be able to do sufficient worship planning; excellent worship planning, however, requires a person who understands the intersection of all the disciplines that make up worship.

As a unique art form, worship has its own unique demands. More than slots filled with musical elements, it is "a narrative (the content moves as a story with inner cohesion)—not a program (a series of isolated and unconnected acts of worship appearing without connection)."[1] Worship requires both quality content and satisfying structure. In some ways worship planning is similar to composition or playwriting in that it is an art form that unfolds over time; therefore, it uses similar artistic devices—structure, flow, repetition, contrast, and development (which are discussed later in this chapter).

However, unlike the composer or playwright, the worship planner is not the ultimate creator of the artistic product. Instead, the Holy Spirit is the director of true worship.[2] The worship planner's creativity lies in discerning the movement of the Spirit, shaping the elements, and providing structure that allows the congregation to respond to God's revelation.

Understanding Service Structure

While some Christians dismiss the idea of worship structure as the domain of formal, liturgical churches, the reality is that every church's worship has structure. This is as it should be. Humans naturally respond to the rhythms of form and order and are more able to comprehend worship content when their attention is not diverted to deciphering endless structural variations. Structural novelty soon frustrates the worshiper—and reveals the whims of the leadership rather than the leading of the Spirit. Instead, variety and spontaneity are channeled into—and given meaning within—a worship structure.

The first task of the worship planner, especially one who is attempting to introduce new music styles and worship expressions, is to understand the existing worship structure. Though there are many treatises that categorize worship structures,[3] for our purposes we will narrow them down into three general categories: Liturgical, Thematic, and Experiential.

Liturgical Worship Structure

The word *liturgical* has many meanings. Strictly speaking it means "the work of the people," but more often it connotes a church with a formal worship style and a predetermined worship structure. Here we will use the word to indicate the historic pattern of Gathering, Word, Table, and Dismissal. This "fourfold pattern of worship," as Robert Webber calls it, has roots in Scripture (see Isaiah 6, Luke 24:13–35, Acts 2:42), precedence in the early church, and broad ecumenical consensus. While it is not a biblical mandate, it is certainly a biblical implication and should be considered normative for worship. In the words of Nicholas Wolterstorff:

> During the last quarter century or so a most remarkable thing has happened: all the mainline traditions of Christendom, with the exception of the Orthodox and the Anabaptist, have engaged in liturgical reform. And even more striking: all the liturgies recommended are virtually identical in structure. Indeed, they are closely similar even in content. There is an emerging liturgical coalescence. If one laid side-by-side the new Catholic, Presbyterian, Reformed, Lutheran, Anglican, Methodist, and other liturgies, the coalescence would be obvious and striking. Once again we can walk into each other's churches and feel at home. The unity of the church has been made concrete; it is there before our eyes and ears.
>
> The person who has not participated in this development will quite naturally suspect that liturgical scholars from these various traditions have been looking over each other's shoulders and copying what they saw. There has been some of that. But the basic dynamic of coalescence has not been that at all. In our century we have once again become acquainted with the liturgy of the church around AD 200—after it had settled in and before it had become encrusted. All the liturgical reform commissions have felt compelled to return to the structure of the liturgy of that time, enriched by a few additions from later Catholicism and later Protestantism. In my judgment we must regard this emergent coalescence as nothing less than a work of the Spirit.[4]

Word and Table balanced. A number of characteristics of the fourfold pattern of worship make worship planning substantially different for a Liturgical service than in a Thematic or Experiential worship structure. The first is that the importance of the Word (preaching) and Table (communion) are balanced. Whereas a Thematic service is dominated by preaching and all other worship elements serve it, the Liturgical service takes the shape of a large arch that slowly builds to the Word and Table, creating a plateau climax rather than the single climactic peak of the Thematic service. The immediate effect of this shape is to pull the sermon back into the context of the overall worship service, unlike the Thematic service in which the sermon creates the context. Second, a more subtle, yet perhaps more important result of this arch form, at least as far as the worship planner is concerned, is that the importance of all the worship elements is heightened. Songs, psalms, and prayers are no longer seen simply as ways to prepare people's hearts for the sermon; they are an essential part of the ongoing worship dialogue.

Revelation and response. Unlike sermon-driven worship in which the main act of the congregation is listening to a lecture-style exposition of Scripture, or music-driven worship in which the people spend most of their time adoring the Lord, the Liturgical model is a constant volley of God revealing himself to the people through the Spirit and the people responding in faith. God reveals his majesty and holiness, and the people respond with confession; God answers the people's confession with an assurance of forgiveness, and the people respond with a song of praise.

Specific texts are required. In Liturgical worship, particular texts are used for particular parts of the worship service or at a particular time of the year. Therefore, the *Sanctus* (Holy, Holy, Holy, Lord God of hosts, etc.) must always be a *Sanctus*—the music style may vary, but the text may not. These liturgical requirements significantly shape the planning process and the song repertoire.

Music fits structure. When planning worship in an Experiential service structure, "the first thing you should think about . . . is not the lyrics, or sermon theme, but on the way you want the room to 'feel' at various places in the service."[5] In contrast, in the Liturgical structure the worship planner doesn't have the freedom to choose music based primarily on its feel or musical flow. Instead, the music fits into the preexisting dramatic flow of the liturgy itself.

Thematic Worship Structure

The Thematic worship structure is a sermon-dominated service that has its roots in the Reformation and nineteenth-century evangelistic revivals. In the Reformation, reason was elevated over (and against) the mystery and faith of the Middle Ages. This new focus on reason, combined with the invention of the printing press, paved the way for a new word-based society in which faith was something to be understood by the individual rather than accepted blindly by the masses.

All the reformers restored the preaching of the Word to a place of esteem within worship, but Ulrich Zwingli in particular elevated the preaching to such a place of prominence that all other elements of worship either were eliminated or served the preaching. Since that time, there has always been a "dissenting" or "free" tradition in which formal liturgy is disdained—any worship elements that remain are seen as preparation for the primary focus of the service, the preaching.

In the nineteenth century, this heritage emerged in a slightly different context in the evangelistic revivals of Dwight L. Moody and others. Here the preaching was an invitation to salvation and the music preceding it was "bait" to entice sinners to the meeting. These parachurch outreach crusades eventually became a paradigm for Sunday worship, especially in the United States, where the first half of the service became somewhat more formalized (call to worship, special music, offering, etc.), the second half was dominated by the sermon, and the service often concluded with an altar call as a response to the preaching.

The significance of this history to the worship planner is twofold. First, the nineteenth-century evangelistic revivals were the first time music had been used to satisfy people's taste. (Luther had adapted music to people's ability to understand, but always in the context of the liturgy and the tradition.) William Booth of the Salvation Army and others used the popular music styles of their day, even rewording the hits of Stephen Foster and others in order to draw in the lost with familiar sounds. This Pandora's box of personal taste now permeates modern worship. Congregations—not only those with revivalist roots—expect music that will appeal to them, usually meaning music similar to the secular pop music of the day.

Second, every worship element in the Thematic worship model serves the preaching. The hymns support the preaching theme, the special music prepares the preaching theme, and even the benediction can be a summary of the preaching theme ("O Lord, help us to be a faithful people who *learn*, *love*, and *live* throughout the coming week"). Any element that doesn't directly reinforce the theme is considered either poor planning or preamble. For example, observe the difference between a psalm reading in Liturgical and Thematic worship. In the liturgical church, the psalm is part of the lectionary (a three-year cycle of Scripture) readings for the day; it is a required part of the service order that is an important part of the scriptural ascent to the Gospel reading. In the Thematic service, the psalm is entirely optional (unless it is the preaching text), it is often chosen for its utility (a call to worship, for instance), and it is frequently used as filler between other elements, such as when it is spoken over an instrumental transition between hymns. The end result is that the psalm carries its own weight within the Liturgical structure, whereas in the Thematic service it is "worship wallpaper." This is true of many other elements as well.

Of course, this shouldn't imply that the Thematic service structure is faulty or deficient. The Thematic form is commendable in that it leads the worshiper forward in a clear fashion. The task of the worship planner in this format is to create a "funnel" that builds toward the service's goal: the sermon. Starting with songs and Scripture passages of general praise, the worship planner slowly narrows the focus, providing special music, hymns, and dramatic sketches that prepare people for the sermon. At the conclusion of the sermon, the worship planner either has appropriate music ready for an altar call or a concluding hymn that drives home the preaching theme.

Experiential Service Structure

The term *Experiential service structure* here denotes those services that are emotional, music driven, and shaped primarily by the worshiper's response rather than a preaching theme or liturgical requirements. It is a by-product of neo-Pentecostal movements and is most closely associated with the Praise & Worship music genre.

The Pentecostal movement is usually traced back to the Azusa Street revival in Los Angeles, but its roots run much deeper in the soil of American Christianity. The initial impulse for the movement can be found in the theology of the Methodist/Holiness movement, which flourished in late nineteenth-century America. Holiness preachers proclaimed the message of the "second blessing" (salvation being the first), in which the Christian experienced an instantaneous purifying of the heart. It wasn't long before the "second blessing" theology combined with the emotionally charged atmosphere of holiness worship to create the "third blessing," or the baptism in the Holy Spirit, as evidenced by charisms such as speaking in tongues, prophesying, and healing. The first person to experience this third blessing was Agnes Ozman, a student in Charles Parham's Bible school in Topeka, Kansas. She spoke in tongues on the first day of the twentieth century, and in so doing began a revival that traveled to Azusa Street in 1906 and soon spread like wildfire all over the world. In just over one hundred years it has become the second largest of the four major branches of Christianity (Roman Catholic, Pentecostal, Orthodox, and Protestant) and continues to be the fastest-growing branch of Christianity throughout the world.

Not only has Pentecostalism experienced tremendous growth in the last century, it has also exerted tremendous influence on American Christianity as a whole. In 1960 a Charismatic movement began in the Episcopal church, and its influence is still felt in today's Episcopal renewal movement. Roman Catholics experienced a similar Charismatic revival in the late 1960s. Indeed, most mainline denominations have some Charismatic element within their ranks today. In the 1980s one of the most important neo-Pentecostal influences on worship emerged under the teaching of John Wimber. Though distancing themselves from the label "Pentecostal," the Vineyard churches that grew under Wimber's leadership nonetheless adopted many Pentecostal worship traits and are certainly open to the charisms.

Experiential worship focuses on the worshiper's experience. The impact of the Pentecostals and neo-Pentecostals on the American church has been enormous. There has been a broad shift away from the reason-based worship of the Thematic service style that dominated the American worship landscape throughout most of the twentieth century. The focus is now turned to the worshiper's experience and emotional response during worship rather than intellectual training. This has led to a new expressiveness in worship that is indicative of modern worshipers' desire to give themselves wholly to God—mind, body, and spirit. There is also a heightened sense of participation in today's worship that restores Luther's ideal of the priesthood of all believers. However, there can also be negative aspects of this newfound worship experience. Passion's flames can only burn for so long without fuel, and it appears that some worshipers attempt to re-create ecstatic worship experiences week after week without receiving the biblical instruction needed to sustain faith's fire. There is also a decidedly individualistic slant to this type of ecstatic experience that denies the corporate aspect of worship.

Music plays an essential role in shaping Experiential worship. Today's worship is motivated by music. The goal of the Pentecostal service is to personally experience the movement of the Spirit in tongues, healing, being slain in the Spirit, and other charisms. Similarly, the goal of neo-Pentecostal and modern worship is intimacy between God and worshiper. In both cases music plays a pivotal role in creating the atmosphere in which this intimate encounter can happen. Vineyard theology goes so far as to categorize types of music that are conducive to this goal. "Praise" is music in which the worshipers talk to each other *about* God and is also termed "horizontal" music. "Worship" is music in which the worshiper talks *to* God—"vertical" music. (Hence, the musical style associated with this type of worship is named "Praise & Worship.") Two biblical models are used to support this theology, converging the implications of the tabernacle's construction with the actions described in Psalm 100:4 to show the progression from the outer courts (thanksgiving), to the inner courts (praise), to the Holy of Holies (worship).

These models raise the question of whether the Holy of Holies is the intimate personal worship that typically takes place at the end of this music sequence, or the preaching that follows it. An even larger problem with this worship structure is that its theology makes little provision for preaching or the sacraments, because it shapes only the musical part of worship. In fact, John Witvliet argues that the music itself is the "sacrament" in this model.[6] Even worship leaders within the Praise & Worship movement struggle with the dominance of music in worship, as attested by the soul-searching lyrics of Matt Redman's song "The Heart of Worship": "I'll bring you more than a song/for a song in itself is not what you have required."

The Praise & Worship genre. The impact of neo-Pentecostalism can be felt in the new genre of music called "Praise & Worship," which has spread like wildfire in the last fifteen years. The Praise & Worship repertoire has crept into even the most traditional churches, and in many cases has entirely replaced hymnody.[7] While new worship expressions are always a welcome freshening of existing repertoire, the marketing forces of the worship industry are difficult to resist, threatening to eliminate the possibility of any other type of worship music. It is especially distressing to see non-Western churches who view Western Praise & Worship as the soundtrack of revival, rather than finding their own unique worship voice.

Expanded role of worship leader. The worship leader is much more important in the Experiential worship model than in the Liturgical or Thematic. The worship leader is expected to establish rapport with the congregation, lead the musicians, and follow the lead of the Holy Spirit.

Planning music for Experiential worship. Worship planning in the Experiential service structure offers the musician a great deal of freedom. While the preaching is important in this format, it makes no demands of the music thematically or liturgically, so the music planner has almost complete control over the rest of the service. The form of the service tends to be a three-part structure similar to the revivalistic model outlined previously: music, preaching, and ministry time (altar call).

The opening music can fill as much as half the total service time. Because the goal of this time is to lead worshipers into intimate worship, it is important that this music flows well, that it has no abrupt tempo changes or dead spots that will break the mood, and that enough time is allowed for people to enter into the worship atmosphere. A typical opening worship time will start with upbeat songs of praise and thanksgiving, calling one another to worship and singing about God's attributes. In many cases, this time of energetic singing ends with prayer, announcements, or other elements that give the people a short rest. Following this, the mood of the music becomes slower and more introspective, giving the worshipers a chance to express themselves to God one on one. The preaching is next, and in some cases there will be skillful coordination between the worship leader and the pastor so that the transition between the music and sermon is seamless, a technique perhaps learned from African-American worship. Concluding the service is a ministry time, also accompanied by music and singing. This part of the service may include an altar call, healing, and individuals responding to the sermon with prayer, confession, and dedication.

Experiential music techniques. Essentially, this is a worship structure with emotional goals that uses musical means to achieve those goals. Therefore, the worship planner must understand the musical techniques that affect the atmosphere and direction of the worship experience: tempo, key, repetition, and transition.

Tempo is important in the Experiential service structure because it, more than any other factor, determines the music's mood and the listener's response. Fast songs elicit a more energetic response than slow songs, so they are used in the beginning of the service when the people are being called together for joyous praise and thanksgiving. Slower music is used as the corporate praise turns to intimate individual worship.

Similarly, the key signatures of songs play a role in establishing mood. Choosing a few songs in the same key allows the songs to be sung without interruption, letting the worship flow and the mood to be unbroken.

Repetition is another technique for maintaining a particular mood. A sufficient amount of time is required before a mood settles in and the people are able to respond. Repeating a song multiple times allows worshipers to become familiar enough with a song that they can turn from thinking about singing to using the song as their own expression of worship. Of course, a song cannot be repeated indefinitely (unless one believes some critics' definition of Praise & Worship: "three words, two chords, one hour"), so transitions such as modulations are used to smooth the edges between songs.

All of these techniques are, in a sense, manipulative. They are used to elicit an emotional response in the worshiper. While no more manipulative than the skillful use of tempo, key, and word painting in hymnody (or any other music for that matter), these tools should only be used to assist the worshipers, not to control them. It is also vital that these techniques and forms don't become a system repeated without variation week after week—three upbeat songs, prayer, three slower songs ending with an a cappella chorus—because the congregation doesn't start and shouldn't end in the same emotional place every week. Ultimately the Holy Spirit must guide worship while the worship planner simply assists with the details.

Adapting Structure and Style

Although the previous discussion has used general terms to describe and categorize different worship paradigms, it is probably clear how these categories normally take shape in the real world. The Liturgical model describes Anglican, Catholic, and "liturgical renewal" churches that utilize historic music forms as well as post–Vatican II repertoire. The Thematic model describes "traditional" churches such as Presbyterian, Methodist, and other mainline denominations that dominated the religious landscape during the middle of the twentieth century, being particularly influenced by gospel songs. The Experiential model describes Pentecostal and neo-Pentecostal churches that feature Praise & Worship.

Blended Worship

Because of the worship upheavals of the last forty years, the lines between these worship models have been increasingly blurred. Liturgical and Thematic churches are finding elements of the Experiential model creeping into their service structures. Likewise, post–Vatican II liturgical renewals are seeping into Experiential model churches, where historic prayers and liturgical forms are being used in new guises. Robert Webber calls this phenomenon "convergence." The more common term for convergence worship, especially as it relates to musical styles, is *blended* worship.

Arguments against blended worship. Of course, no worship movement is without its detractors, and blended worship is no exception. Critiques of blended worship ("blender" worship, as critics have dubbed it) center primarily on three issues. The first is the "garbage in, garbage out" principle, which claims that any worship coming out of the "blender" will only be as good as the ingredients going in. Critics of blended worship think that lowest common denominator worship elements must necessarily be used in blended worship, and therefore the results will be inferior. Second, they also perceive this "buffet" approach to worship as a way to accommodate selfish and lazy worshipers, destroying the vigor and balance of historic worship traditions. Finally, some argue that musical style is imbued with meaning that can support or distort the theology of worship, and that any allowance for popular musical styles in church, even in the relatively small amounts used in the blended worship paradigm, is a capitulation to a consumeristic culture that betrays the themes of sacrifice and discipline that are integral to the Christian message.[8]

Are the critics right? Is it impossible to contain the new wine of musical styles in the old wineskins of historic worship structures (or vice versa)? No, not impossible, but it certainly requires discernment and skill.

Arguments for blended worship. While it is true that many churches turn to blended worship simply as a way to avoid conflict, a strong argument can be made that blended worship is a biblically and historically sound paradigm. In fact, the whole history of the church's worship has shown an ever-flowing historical river that has constantly been refreshed by modern streams. The most obvious example of this is Martin Luther's reviving of the Roman liturgy with vernacular language and common musical styles, but similar situations can be found as far back as the Israelites' use of neighboring countries' musical and poetic forms. It is an issue that calls for great sensitivity and discernment; too much vernacular influence may allow the medium to overwhelm the message, but rigid adherence to perceived historical purity may drain the worship of its lifeblood. For most churches, the wisest decision is to find a place on the spectrum that gives voice both to the people in the pews and to the saints who have gone before, giving worship both relevance to modern culture and roots in tradition.

Perhaps critics are responding more to the way blended worship is normally practiced in the local church rather than the worship philosophy itself. Indeed, many music ministers lack the theological reflection and musical sensitivity to successfully blend styles, resulting in worship that is a motley collection of elements with no coherence. Bringing worship elements from different eras and traditions together is a delicate task. The key to planning successful blended worship is to compare the structure and intent of the Liturgical, Thematic, and Experiential worship models, identifying which elements must remain intact and which can be transplanted into a new worship environment.

Comparing Worship Models

Comparing structure. The fundamental forms of Thematic and Experiential services are quite similar; both begin with a "song service" (also called a "worship time") that occupies up to half of the service. Though the Thematic may have more prescribed elements and the Experiential may have stronger psychological goals, both have reasonable flexibility with the specific elements that make up this section of the service. Both models continue with the sermon, which is given greater relative importance in the Thematic model.

The largest variation between the Thematic and Experiential comes after the sermon. The Experiential invariably allows for a ministry time—a chance to respond to the Word with further musical worship as well as prayer for forgiveness, healing, or salvation. Some Thematic services, especially those in the evangelical tradition, will allow time after the sermon for an altar call or extended prayer time, while others may end only with a prayer, benediction, or hymn.

Unlike the somewhat flexible three-part structure of the Thematic and Experiential models, the Liturgical model consists of four broad sections—Gathering, Word, Table, and Dismissal—each of which has prescribed elements within it. The more rigid structure of the Liturgical model is not entirely incompatible with the other two models, however. Its broadest gesture is still similar to the Thematic and Experiential models: acts of entering God's presence, experiencing God's presence, and responding to God's presence. These similarities are shown in the graph on page 100.

	Entering God's Presence	Experiencing God's Presence	Responding to God's Presence
Liturgical	Gather | Word	| Table	| Dismissal
Thematic	Song Service	| Sermon	| Altar Call
Experiential	Worship Time |	Sermon |	Ministry Time

Comparing intent. Though the three worship models share similar structures, they reveal significant divergence in their intent, goals, and spirit. The Liturgical model is characterized by a sense of transcendence. Regardless of the musical style, the worshiper in the liturgical church has a sense of taking part in something larger than oneself. It is a submission of the individual will to the will of the church universal, resulting in an objective worship experience—one that some may find emotionally dry and unfulfilling. Unlike the transcendence of the Liturgical model, the Thematic model is firmly rooted in the intellect and reason. Coherence of presentation is valued, and the pedagogical intentions of the paradigm can be so strongly felt that the Thematic model faces the danger of becoming a lecture with no opportunity for the expressive participation of the people. The Experiential model is marked by a spirit of joyous energy that soon gives way to intimate spiritual encounter. However, the quest to provide a relevant experience for the worshiper can lead to a subjective worship atmosphere ruled by feeling and personal taste.

Identifying essential worship elements. Every worship model has elements that are unique or essential to its character. These must be identified and preserved.

The Lord's Supper is the worship element that differentiates the Liturgical model from the others. In the Roman Catholic tradition, the Table is seen as the pivotal act of worship—worship without celebrating the Lord's Supper is like having "appetizers without the meal," as Brennan Manning has quipped. In other liturgical traditions it may not be elevated to quite that extent, but it is certainly an essential component of the worship structure. Beyond the Table there may be other immutable worship actions such as the invocation, confession, and creeds. The style of these elements may change, but if the elements themselves are moved or eliminated, the theology of the service is betrayed.

In the Thematic model, the sermon is the only element of the service that cannot be altered. All other elements may be changed for practical or theological reasons, but the preaching of the Word remains central. Of course, this overlooks the fact that other elements—special music, children's sermons, or opening hymns—may be entrenched traditions that the people in the pews will not let go of lightly.

Long stretches of music are critical to the Experiential model and the key to its psychological impact. Another characteristic of this model is the spontaneity and fluidity of form that usually accompanies the worship. Both the extended praise set and the spontaneous feel of this worship style can be successfully transplanted into other worship models.

Methods of Blending

There are three fundamental methods used to blend together traits of these worship models: modernizing style, substituting elements, and combining structures. We will focus primarily on the blending of Experiential model traits into Liturgical and Thematic structures, as this is the most frequently used technique.

Modernizing style. A modern style of music may often be substituted for a historic one. The Roman Catholic church has been doing this since Vatican II, when the allowance for the liturgy to be sung in local languages and music styles led to an explosion of new liturgical music. Similarly, it is common in Protestant churches to use modern English rather than King James, or to have a traditional hymn led by a worship team. One problem with simply inserting modernized elements into the existing liturgy is that it can lead to an unseemly pastiche of styles. While this type of patchwork approach is more acceptable to a postmodern aesthetic, it is still likely to appear haphazard to most of the congregation.

Substituting elements. Rather than simply inserting a modernized element into the existing structure, one can create a more seamless quality by replacing an existing section with a new one that functions the same way as the old one. For example, some churches replace an instrumental prelude or the opening hymn of praise with a set of praise songs. While these choices certainly affect the mood of the service, the liturgical function is similar. Another common place for the singing of praise music is during communion. It is especially effective to have the congregation singing simple choruses as they walk forward to take the cup and bread, making the experience more communal and participatory than if communion were to be served in the pew while instrumental music plays.

Notice that each of these changes incorporates sets of praise songs rather than individual songs. One of the hallmarks of the Experiential model is the extended praise set. To capture this feel, it is best to sing two or more praise songs at a time. Of course, there are times when individual songs fit the worship setting perfectly (for example, singing a song such as "Purify My Heart" by Jeff Nelson in place of—or in addition to—a confession, or singing a quiet chorus as a response of dedication after the sermon).

Combining structures. Elements can be taken from different worship models and layered in such a way that the existing structure is retained while a secondary structure is superimposed on top of it. A simple example of this would be a Thematic structure that takes on an Experiential-style worship time in the first half of the service. Because the two structures are so similar, this is more a change of style than substance. Perhaps to retain the Thematic intent of this model, the service could start with general praise and then move in a funnel shape toward the sermon theme. Often in this scenario, the momentum of worship can slow down to the point that a pre-sermon hymn is just the right transition from worship music to preaching. This same worship plan would be flexible enough to retain specific elements that were essential to the church's existing worship structure. For example, if a spoken element such as a call to worship or the reading of a psalm were to be retained, it could be spoken as the worship team transitions to the next song, retaining both the specific worship element from the Thematic structure and the free-flowing style of the Experiential structure. Of course, overusing this technique can send the signal to the congregation that the Scripture passage is "filler" and that musical flow is the real priority.

Another example of structural convergence is using what I call a psalm "sequence" rather than reading a psalm in unison or responsively. A psalm sequence takes a psalm and breaks it into logical sections, adding music around it to create a psalm-driven worship set. This is not only a way to give a Thematic or Liturgical structure a more modern Experiential style but also an excellent way of weaving the psalms into the fabric of the Experiential structure (which is too often lacking in the use of Scripture). One could go a step further and tie together a psalm sequence with other elements in a Liturgical service such as the confession and assurance.

The following is an example showing a section of a Liturgical service (based on a Reformed worship model) that uses a psalm sequence in a modern music style. Observe how the psalm sequence is a flowing medley of song and Scripture, typical of the Praise & Worship context, which fulfills the mandates of the given Liturgical structure.

Liturgical structure (beginning only)	**Psalm sequence** (based on structure to the left)
Call to Worship	Unison reading: *O Lord, open my lips, and my mouth will declare your praise.* (Psalm 51:15)
Hymn	"O Splendor of God's Glory Bright" "Here I Am to Worship" "Create in Me" (starts quietly)
Prayer of Confession	Leader reads over instrumental music: *Have mercy on me, O God, according to your unfailing love; according to your great compassion blot out my transgressions. Wash away all my iniquity and cleanse me from my sin.* *For I know my transgressions, and my sin is always before me. Against you, you only, have I sinned and done what is evil in your sight, so that you are proved right when you speak and justified when you judge.* *Surely I was sinful at birth, sinful from the time my mother conceived me. Surely you desire truth in the inner parts; you teach me wisdom in the inmost place.* *Cleanse me with hyssop, and I will be clean; wash me, and I will be whiter than snow. Let me hear joy and gladness; let the bones you have crushed rejoice. Hide your face from my sins and blot out all my iniquity.* (Psalm 51:1–9)

People sing: "Create in Me a Clean Heart"

Unison reading: *The sacrifices of God are a broken spirit; a broken and contrite heart, O God, you will not despise.* (Psalm 51:17)

Assurance of Pardon   People sing: "Create in Me a Clean Heart"

Next is an example of a Thematic service, united by a passage from Isaiah 6 and carried out in the style of a flowing set of Praise & Worship.

Thematic structure	**Theme: Isaiah 6:1–8**
Opening Hymn	"We Come to Praise You" "He Is Exalted" "Lord, I Lift Your Name on High"
Call to Worship	Leader: *In the year that King Uzziah died, I saw the Lord seated on a throne, high and exalted, and the train of his robe filled the temple. Above him were seraphs, each with six wings: With two wings they covered their faces, with two they covered their feet, and with two they were flying. And they were calling to one another:* People: *"Holy, holy, holy is the Lord Almighty; the whole earth is full of his glory."* Leader: *At the sound of their voices the doorposts and thresholds shook and the temple was filled with smoke.* (Isaiah 6:1–4)
Hymn, Special Music, Offering	"Holy, Holy, Holy" (verses 1 and 2) "Throw Down Your Crowns" "We Bow Down" Leader (over music): *"Woe to me!" I cried. "I am ruined! For I am a man of unclean lips, and I live among a people of unclean lips, and my eyes have seen the King, the Lord Almighty."* (Isaiah 6:5) "Holy, Holy, Holy" (verse 3 a cappella)
Pastoral Prayer	Pastoral Prayer (perhaps focusing on the themes of confession and forgiveness that are found in the readings from Isaiah) Leader: *Then one of the seraphs flew to me with a live coal in his hand, which he had taken with tongs from the altar. With it he touched my mouth and said, "See, this has touched your lips; your guilt is taken away and your sin atoned for."* (Isaiah 6:6–7)
Pre-Sermon Hymn	"Holy, Holy, Holy" (verse 4, with descant)
Sermon	Sermon: "A Vision of God's Holiness"
Song of Commitment	Leader: *Then I heard the voice of the Lord saying, "Whom shall I send? And who will go for us?" And I said,* People: *"Here am I. Send me!"* (Isaiah 6:8) "Here I Am, Lord"

These examples require a certain amount of flexibility from the existing worship structure because they follow the spirit of the structure rather than the exact details. There may not be as much room for experimentation in a highly structured worship environment such as the Roman Catholic mass. Otherwise, the possibilities for structural convergence are limited only by the worship planner's imagination.

Practical Worship-Planning Techniques

It is one thing to have ideas about how to adapt your worship structure to accommodate new styles of music; it is another to have the hands-on skills needed to plan excellent worship services. Here are some practical techniques necessary for planning worship, with special attention paid to the development and flow that characterize modern worship.

Shaping Themes

Shaping scriptural, musical, and emotional themes is important because it engages the worshiper and clarifies the worship experience. To understand how the shaping of artistic materials affects a participant's experience, consider Beethoven's Symphony No. 5. The opening theme—da, da, da, dum (G, G, G, E♭)—is the hammer blow that begins and holds together the entire musical *tour de force* that follows. The theme is then immediately repeated a step lower (F, F, F, D). Beethoven could have repeated the sequence once more (E♭, E♭, E♭, C—potentially finishing on the tonic of C with a very short symphony), but instead he chooses to develop the theme in a lighter, more lyrical style. Throughout the symphony, Beethoven keeps the listener in his grip by bringing back the theme in different contexts and guises. Each new appearance of the theme is surrounded by enough contrasting material to make it feel like the return of an old friend. Beethoven leads us on a journey, and we gladly take part in the theme's growth, development, and transformation. In the same way, the worship planner invites the worshiper into a story—the gospel story. And just like any artist, the worship planner uses the tools of repetition, contrast, and development to shape the material.

Repetition. Some church leaders give the impression that creative, engaging worship results from constant innovation—each moment must be unique and new or the worshiper will become bored. On the contrary, God has wired the mind to search for repeated patterns in the world, and whether these are patterns in time (day and night) or place (land and sea), they give meaning to the human experience. The same is true of worship. Even if it were possible to craft a worship service without repetition, the resulting lack of coherence would dumbfound the congregation. Instead, the worship planner seeks ways to introduce and reintroduce themes that will deepen the impact of worship.

Musical themes can be repeated in much the same way that Beethoven introduces a theme and develops it throughout a symphony. For example, "Brethren, We Have Met to Worship" could be used as an opening hymn, and "God, the Father of Your People," which uses the same tune (Holy Manna), could close the service, creating "bookends" that provide emotional closure. A tune could also be brought back throughout the service as Marty Haugen does with the tune "Santo, Santo, Santo" (holy, holy, holy) for all of the congregational responses in "Santo: Eucharistic Acclamations" (GIA G-5813).

Textual repetition can be used to shape service themes. For example, the regal hymn "Holy, Holy, Holy" (Nicaea) could be followed by the sweet Argentinean song "Santo, Santo, Santo" mentioned above to allow the worshiper to experience the holiness of God from two different perspectives. Another example of textual repetition is a set of songs all exploring a theme like "bowing down," a name for God such as "Emmanuel," or a phrase like "Ancient of Days."

There is also the use of multiple verbatim repetitions, such as those practiced by Taizé to lead to a meditative atmosphere or in Pentecostal worship to bring on an ecstatic spiritual state. While these are valid uses of repetition, the worship planner should use them with care, because they require or create a particular atmosphere that may be incongruent with the typical Sunday morning worship.

Contrast. Contrast provides the vehicle for thematic growth within worship in the same way that conflict fuels a novel's plot. For example, the Reformed liturgy moves from a hymn of adoration to congregational confession, a contrast that drives home the message that God is holy and we are not. Our only response when entering God's presence is to confess our sinfulness. Contrast is apparent in a salvation message that starts with God's judgment and ends with his mercy. There can also be effective use of contrasting musical styles such as singing the heavy, objective, minor key hymn "O the Deep, Deep Love of Jesus" (Ebenezer) followed by the simple, first-person children's song "Jesus Loves Me." Of course, one must be careful that the contrasts used are meaningful rather than contrived.

Development. Development is, in a sense, the result of repetition and contrast. Christians are called to be transformed into new creatures (Rom. 12:2). Development within the worship service mirrors and initiates this spiritual growth. Most worship services include aspects of development within the liturgy itself; for example, the change in perspective from the individual to the corporate as we enter worship, or moving from hearing the Word to living the Word as we leave worship. The Vineyard model of worship displays development in its journey from thanksgiving, to praise, to adoration.

Development can be initiated by musical choices as well. A song can come back in different styles or instrumentation throughout a service to mark the worship journey that is taking place. For example, a jubilant rendition of "Come, Thou Fount of Every Blessing" can start the worship service, and the third verse ("O to grace how great a debtor") can return in a slower and more reflective musical style during the confession and assurance or the communion. Of course, the sermon is another important aspect of leading the worshiper from one place to another.

Enhancing Flow

Entering into worship that is riddled with stops, starts, breaks, interruptions, and awkward pauses is difficult. The worship planner should seek to enhance the flow of worship by identifying dynamic and static worship elements and connecting or buffering these elements appropriately.

108   The Art of worship

Dynamic elements. Dynamic worship elements are those things that naturally lead to another; inherent in their nature is forward motion. For example, when a liturgist addresses the congregation with "Peace be with you," it automatically leads to the congregation replying, "And also with you." Another strongly dynamic element is Praise & Worship music. Songs in this style are more or less created to be sung in medleys, so each song feels incomplete by itself and implies a segue into another song.

Static elements. On the other hand, static elements dissipate forward motion to greater or lesser degrees. For instance, announcements are static—any energy or momentum that was built during worship will be entirely undermined by a time of announcements, and then new energy will have to be expended to put the service in motion again. Other examples of worship elements that are static to some extent are children's sermons, special music, and preaching.

Dynamic and *static* are not terms that indicate the quality or importance of a particular element, only the amount of momentum it adds to a service. Preaching is an excellent and necessary part of worship, yet it would be labeled static because the emotional flow of worship is suspended as the people settle into a stationary posture of hearing. This is not the case in African-American worship where the sermon is a verbal volley between the preacher and people, maintaining a high level of energy and momentum. The extent to which any element of worship will take on a dynamic or static role depends on the church and the placement and presentation of the element. It is the job of the worship planner to identify which elements are dynamic and which are static in his or her own context, and then skillfully arrange the elements into an ebb and flow of energy that engages worshipers.

Connecting elements. Joining worship elements together creates larger worship segments, allowing the worshiper more time and opportunity to step into the unfolding worship drama. In practice this may mean smoothing the transition between a hymn and a praise song by choosing songs in the same key—on the last note of the hymn, the worship team begins their introduction. It may be an instrumental transition from one song to the next, or something as simple as planning for a speaker to be in place with the microphone turned on so the person can begin speaking without waiting or feeling the compulsion to tap the microphone and ask if it's on.

Buffering elements. Of course, not all worship elements can be connected to each other, nor should they be. It is important to buffer static elements from other elements in order to avoid jarring transitions between different energy levels. A service that moves from singing "I Will Celebrate" to a death announcement to an upbeat gospel anthem by the choir puts worshipers on an emotional roller coaster. A better way of including the death announcement is to group it with the morning prayer; it will then be congruent with its surroundings and the people can respond to the announcement in a helpful and appropriate way—through prayer. Worship elements do not normally vary so wildly in energy level as the example above (and most worship planners have the presence of mind to avoid ordering them in such a way), but all worship planners will inevitably be forced to juggle a number of disparate elements on any given Sunday: testimonies, special music, announcements, new member introductions, and mission updates. The key is to arrange them in such a way that there is a natural ebb and flow between high and low energy, a balance of sung and spoken elements, and the assurance that the people are not standing or sitting for too long.

Consider the possibilities for connecting and buffering the following elements: choral anthem, hymn, missionary report, praise set, prayer, and preaching. One possibility would be to use the choral anthem as a call to worship, followed by a praise set, ending with a slower, missions-oriented song; after the missionaries speak, the pastor begins his prayer by praying for the missionaries; the people sing a hymn related to the sermon theme before they hear the sermon. This type of flow creates an organic experience that does not fatigue or jolt the congregation.

Using Instrumentation for Cohesion and Variety

Similar to the thematic repetition and contrast discussed previously, instruments can be used to create unity of texture (cohesion) or refreshing contrasts (variety). Worship in many churches includes a variety of ensembles—worship team, choir, organ, and orchestra—but often their involvement in the service is entirely separate from one another. While there are many practical reasons for these divisions of labor—different repertoire, scheduling issues, disparate styles—it is desirable to bring together these musical forces as frequently as possible in order to create musical unity within each service as well as a sense of shared purpose in the music ministry.

Cohesion. Instrumental cohesion can be achieved in many ways. The choir can contribute a descant or harmony to a praise song or hymn. The organ can play simple, sustained chords during a praise song, giving a richer texture than a synthesizer could provide. The rhythm section of the worship team can add a light rhythmic accompaniment to a hymn. Ecclesiastes 4:12 says that "a cord of three strands is not quickly broken," and this principle applies to worship as well—when the many strands of musicians are braided together, the result is a stronger overall worship experience.

Variety. This is not to say that constant activity from all the ensembles is the goal. Indeed, this kind of monochromatic instrumentation quickly becomes tiresome. Instead, identify which instrument or ensemble is the most appropriate leader for each song and allow the lead and complementary instruments to flow naturally from song to song. For example, in a set of three songs that are all in the same key, the key provides the cohesion, so there is opportunity for instrumental variety: the piano leads on the first song, the guitar on the second, and the organ on the third. Another possibility is to utilize a cappella singing as a relief from constant instrumental texture. Even within the same song different instrumentation can be used. For example, the worship team could lead the first two verses of a song while quiet fingerpicked guitar leads verse three; on verse four the worship team returns, and organ and a trumpet descant are added. Here, as elsewhere, imagination and taste are used to create a natural ebb and flow that freshens the worship without being a distraction to the worshiper.

Modulation

Modulations from one key to the next provide emotional lift and, more important for the purposes of increasing flow, allow seamless transitions within praise sets.

Modulate within a song, rather than between songs. If the goal is to achieve a seamless set of music, the break between songs presents an obvious problem. Certainly, an instrumentalist can modulate and transition between songs of different keys so that there is no cessation of sound, but there are still two seams that can emphasize the break: a song transition and a key change. However, a modulation during the first song allows it to conclude in the same key as the second, distributing the seams evenly throughout the set of songs (provided that the keys of two adjacent songs are no more than a step apart and the vocal range of the first song is conducive to a key change). Imagine each key change or song transition as a step: a modulation between songs means a two-step jump, whereas a modulation during the song allows one step to be taken at a time.

Plan modulations. Song key is an important factor in worship planning; it is not as important as lyric function and song quality, but when two songs are appropriate, choose the one with a key that is conducive to flow. For this reason, the prepared worship planner should memorize or catalog the keys of the songs in his or her repertoire, as well as the vocal ranges of the songs, in order to be aware of the modulatory possibilities in any combination of songs. Those worship teams whose decision making occurs while actually leading worship may want to predetermine a modulation formula for spur of the moment modulations. For example, the team may decide to always modulate up by a half or whole step. A guitar-oriented band may choose to go to the nearest guitar-friendly key: E, (F), G, A, (B), C, or D. A band with trumpets and saxes may stay with flat keys: E♭, F, G♭, A♭, B♭, C, D♭.

Smoothing Sections

Once the structure of the worship service has been established, make final adjustments—usually during rehearsal—to smooth any remaining gaps between elements.

Transitions. A verbal transition may be needed to make the development of a particular section clear. A musical transition may be added under a verbal element. Song introductions and codas may need to be shortened or lengthened depending on how elements time out in rehearsal. For example, when transitioning into a new or difficult song, use a longer introduction to establish key, tempo, and melody. When transitioning between two very similar songs such as Carl Tuttle's "Hosanna" and Rich Mullins's "O God, You Are My God," you may need no transition or introduction at all.

Eliminate dead air. Much attention should be devoted to eliminating unintentional silence or "dead air" as it is called in radio. Nothing crushes momentum like the seemingly eternal wait as a speaker meanders to a microphone, a liturgist tries to remember what part of the service they're in, or the worship team decides who will begin the next song. This is not only a momentum problem, it also draws attention to the mechanics of worship rather than the Object of worship, and it creates insecurity in the worshiping body.

Of course, *silence* is very different from dead air and should be a regular element in worship. Too many churches, especially in a modern worship style, make no provision for the worshiper to hear the "still small voice" of the Lord. As Marilyn Chandler McEntyre puts it:

> The church's long history of contemplative practice seems to suggest that there is some knowledge of God that can come only in stillness—silence large and long and intentional enough to open a sacred space for the Holy One to enter. To fill up that silence—even with what seems harmless, hospitable chatter or with the preoccupations of perpetual responsibility—forecloses some possibility of intimate encounter with the Word who speaks in "sheer silence."[9]

Rehearse transitions. Transitions should occupy the bulk of the rehearsal time. Remember that the goal is to assist the congregation's worship; an intricate drum beat and exciting saxophone fills won't make or break the worship experience, but awkward pauses, fumbled modulations, and poorly established tempos will.

Modulation Types

There are a number of different types of modulations. Though it is sufficient to simply use the dominant chord of the new key for every modulation, knowing all the modulatory possibilities increases the worship planner's creative options.

Utilitarian Pop Modulation

By far the most frequently used modulation, the Utilitarian Pop Modulation is commendable because it is simple to perform and effective in almost every situation. To modulate to the next key, a dominant chord (the chord built on the fifth scale degree) of the new key is inserted into the measure before the new key. For example, to modulate from the key of F to the key of G, a D (or D7) chord is used to prepare the new key (ex. 1a). This modulation technique is simple enough that a whole band can execute it without any explanation or rehearsal. It is also such a quick and nondescript modulation that it draws very little attention to itself.

Example 1a **Utilitarian Pop Modulation**; "All in All" (F to G)

Two useful variations may be used to soften this transition. The first is the suspension of the third of the new dominant (V) chord (ex. 1b). Modulating from F to G, a Dsus (i.e., a D chord with a G instead of F#) is used immediately before the D preparation chord. The effect of the suspended transition is smoother because it doesn't jump directly to the note that is most foreign to the old key (F#).

Example 1b **Utilitarian Pop Modulation, suspended**

The second variation is the bass "walk down" (ex. 1c). Once again modulating from the key of F to the key of G, an E is used to fill in the scale between F (the old tonic, or I chord) and D (the new dominant, or V chord), instilling a sense of forward motion and inevitability into the progression.

Example 1c **Utilitarian Pop Modulation, bass walk down**

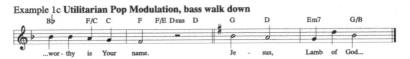

A bass "walk up" can also be added between the new dominant and new tonic (D, E, F#, G) (ex. 1d).

Example 1d **Utilitarian Pop Modulation, bass walk up**

Motivic Modulation

The Motivic Modulation is most frequently used by organists who are modulating into the final verse of a hymn and by pianists who have an extended period to transition from one song to another. There is no simple formula for this type of modulation. Instead there are some common principles that guide the musician's thinking. The first principle is to use the melodic materials of the song as a basis for the modulation. Motives or motivic fragments are linked together, repeated, and developed in such a way that they lead to new tonal areas. Every song has different themes and therefore suggests different treatments. Below is just one example of the way themes can be used to lead to new keys (ex. 2). The second principle is to begin the motivic development quickly, preferably

Example 2 **Motivic Modulation**; "All in All" (F to G)

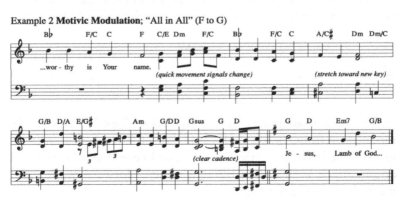

while the congregation is still singing their last note, to signal that they shouldn't dive right into the next verse. It is also important that the modulation end with a clear cadence in the new key that signals the congregation to begin singing again. Third, the accidentals used in the modulation should stretch toward the new key. In example 2 the modulation moves from a flat key (F) to a sharp key (G). In order to fully prepare the new key, the modulation quickly leans toward sharps—even overshooting the target key by using C#s and G#s—so that when the new key arrives it feels natural and settled. Because of the demands of this type of modulation, many musicians will want to plan or even write out the modulation.

Unprepared Modulation

As its name connotes, the Unprepared Modulation forgoes the typical modulation's transitional material and dominant chord that ordinarily establishes the new key. Instead, it jumps right to the new key without preparation. This sudden shift in tonality can be exciting or confusing depending on how skillfully it is implemented. The Unprepared Modulation is most effective with a song that starts after the downbeat, as in "I Believe in Jesus" (ex. 3a). This gives the congregation a moment to hear the new key before singing. This modulation can be aided by a change in texture such as a crescendo, a drum fill, or even complete silence, which cues the congregation that a change of some type is about to take place.

Example 3a **Unprepared Modulation**; "I Believe in Jesus" (E to F)

One way to give the congregation information about the new key, while not giving away the surprise of the sudden tonal shift, is to suspend the fourth of the old key's tonic (I) chords. As shown in example 3b, the old key's fourth is the new key's third. Of course, this works only with songs that modulate up a half step and is particularly effective with melodies that begin on the third.

Example 3b **Unprepared Modulation with Suspension**; "We Fall Down" (E to F)

Example 4 **Tag Modulation**; "How Majestic" (C to D)

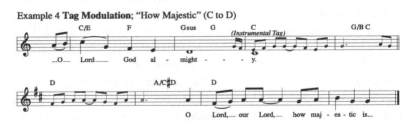

Tag Modulation

The Tag Modulation is, in a sense, a combination of the Motivic and Unprepared Modulations, preparing the new key with a sudden shift to a transposed motive or melodic fragment. For example, the most striking theme of Michael W. Smith's "How Majestic" is the opening melody with the words, "O Lord, our Lord, how majestic is Your name in all the earth." This can be sequenced as a short preparation for the new key (ex. 4). As with all modulations, the transitional material must precede the congregation's normal entrance in order to alert them to wait for their entrance in a new key.

Deceptive Modulation

The Deceptive Modulation uses a deceptive cadence (V-vi instead of the typical V-I) to lead to the new key. Because the ear is already familiar with deceptive cadences from their abundant use in song tags, it is logical and natural to use this musical device to stretch toward a new key. The first step in creating a Deceptive Modulation is to substitute a vi chord for the I chord that normally ends a song. In example 5a, we see that the vi chord harmonizes the last melody note perfectly and also initiates movement into a new key.

Example 5a **Deceptive Modulation**; "How Majestic" (C) to "Lord, I Lift Your Name on High" (G)

Another interesting Deceptive Modulation uses a major VI chord rather than the typical minor vi. The major VI (usually suspended) provides a refreshing twist to what the ear expects and also allows movement into new tonal areas. In example 5b a suspended major VI chord in the key of C (A) is used to pivot into the key of D. Notice that the last note of the melody was altered to fit the chord—this may confuse the congregation, so this modulation may be more safely implemented as an instrumental tag after the congregation finishes the melody.

Example 5b **Deceptive Modulation, suspended major VI**; "How Majestic" (C to D)

The Deceptive Modulation can also stay right in the key of the deceptive major chord. In example 5c, a suspended major VI in C (Asus) simply resolves into the new key of A.

Example 5c **Deceptive Modulation, suspended major VI**; "How Majestic" (C) to "Shout to the Lord" (A)

Picardy Modulation

The Picardy Modulation uses the so-called "Picardy Third" to modulate from a minor to a major key. This cadence has been used so frequently throughout music history that the ear is not at all surprised to hear its characteristic major third at the conclusion of a minor key song. In example 6, "Humble Thyself" in E minor concludes on a major E chord, which becomes the tonic chord of "Come, Let Us Worship and Bow Down" in E major.

Example 6 **Picardy Modulation**; "Humble Thyself" (Em) to "Come, Let Us Worship" (E)

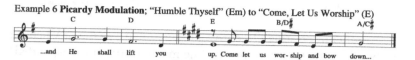

Relative Key Modulation

Major and minor keys that have the same number of sharps or flats are called relative keys. They are so closely related that a transitional chord is all that is needed to smooth the modulation. For example, in example 7a "Good to Me" in G major modulates to "O the Deep, Deep Love of Jesus" in E minor by simply inserting a D/F# chord between the two songs. Notice that the V of the old key is used instead of the dominant B chord that would normally be used to prepare the key of E minor. Because the keys are so closely related, there is no need to use the more abrupt B chord.

Example 7a **Relative Key Modulation**; "Good to Me" (G) to "O the Deep, Deep Love of Jesus" (Em)

The same type of transition can be used when moving from a minor to its related major key, as shown in example 7b.

Example 7b **Relative Key Modulation**; "O the Deep, Deep Love of Jesus" (Em) to "Good to Me" (G)

Pivot Tone Modulation

The Pivot Tone Modulation uses a common tone to connect two often distantly related keys. The result is an arresting shift to a new key like those heard in romantic era classical music and Broadway musicals. Example 8a shows one possibility: "We Exalt Thee" in the key of F ends on the tonic note and chord (F), then uses the common tone A to pivot into the key of D. The modulation is entirely consonant harmonically because the A pivot is the third of the F chord as well as the fifth of the new key of D, yet the effect is surprising because of the sudden shift to a distant tonal area.

Example 8a **Pivot Tone Modulation**; "We Exalt Thee" (F to D)

Of course, not all songs include a repeated melody note such as this that offers an easy way to pivot to a new key. In example 8b a series of tones is used to pivot between keys in the song "Be Exalted." The melody of "Be Exalted" begins with the first three notes of a major scale over a tonic (I) chord. The modulation is accomplished by moving this three-note sequence up a third, bringing in the new key on the last note of the sequence. Granted, this alters the melodic sequence, but the change is so momentary that the congregation will quickly stabilize in the new key.

Example 8b **Pivot Tone Modulation**; "Be Exalted" (G to B♭)

Pivot Chord Modulation

Similar to the Pivot Tone Modulation, the Pivot Chord Modulation uses a chord common to both keys to smoothly join the two together. Example 9a shows "Come, Let Us Worship and Bow Down" in the key of D transitioning easily into "Shine, Jesus, Shine" in A by using the A chord that is common to both keys. Because this modulation doesn't require motivic manipulation, it is quite possible for a pianist or guitarist to use this technique without preparation in a live setting. The technique is made even easier when one understands that closely related keys (one sharp or flat away from each other) share two major chords. For instance, the key of D and the key of A both include D and A chords.

Example 9a **Pivot Chord Modulation**; "Come, Let Us Worship and Bow Down" (D)
to "Shine, Jesus, Shine" (A)

A common variation on the Pivot Chord Modulation is one that exchanges the subdominant (IV) and dominant (V) to modulate a step down. Most melodies end on the first scale degree over a tonic (I) chord. A subdominant (IV) chord can therefore be substituted to harmonize this final note, and the IV chord can become the V chord in a new key one step lower. In example 9b, "Come, Let Us Worship and Bow Down" in the key of D ends on the G chord, which becomes the dominant (V) in the new key of C. As stated previously, modulations almost always proceed to higher keys. However, this step down modulation is useful, for example, when introducing a new song in a key that is comfortable to a soloist and then modulating down for comfortable congregational singing.

Example 9b **Pivot Chord Modulation**, IV-V Exchange; "Come, Let Us Worship and Bow Down" (D to C)

5

MAKING MUSIC

The Role of the Worship Team

When one considers Praise & Worship, it is almost impossible to imagine it without the "worship team." The worship team is to modern worship what the organ was to American worship fifty years ago. Where once it was shocking to see a guitar in the sanctuary, today it is common to have guitar, bass, drums, synthesizer, piano, and a full complement of microphones and monitors. This list of equipment should make it clear what has happened—today's worship is led by a rock band. A tame version with twice as many vocalists as NSYNC, but a rock band nonetheless.

Is the Worship Team Necessary?

Many have questioned the necessity of this change in musical leadership—can't new musical styles be led by existing ensembles? While there is surely room for worship teams to loosen their grip to allow other ensembles to lead worship, there are three reasons that worship teams play a unique and important role in leading Praise & Worship music.

121

1. Stylistic authenticity. In the same way that the organ is not the first choice for leading an African worship song, the organ is not the first choice for the Praise & Worship genre. Praise & Worship is, when all is said and done, a derivative of rock and pop music. Therefore, it is most authentic to have a rock/pop band lead this music style when it is used in worship.

2. Agile leadership. Worship teams provide a unique form of leadership to the congregation. Their rhythmic backbone coupled with a relatively small group of singers creates an agile ensemble that can effectively guide the congregation in the syncopations and variations of form that are part of the Praise & Worship style. Also, there tends to be a higher rate of song introductions in this area of a church's repertoire, and the focused leadership of the worship team can give the clear guidance the congregation needs. Of course, there are some who react negatively to this type of up-front, "in your face" leadership. The worship team should lead and assist the congregation without becoming an overbearing stage presence.

3. Essential accompaniment. Worship teams are important in the Praise & Worship style because they play the essential musical role of rhythmic and chordal accompaniment. This is perhaps made clear by contrasting Praise & Worship to hymnody. Hymns are a self-sufficient form, in that the four vocal parts shown in the hymnal can be sung entirely by the congregation. These four parts are the only essential elements needed to effectively perform the style—it is self-accompanying. Granted, there is normally some accompanying instrument—organ, piano, orchestra—but this is only a doubling of the existing vocal lines rather than an irreplaceable accompaniment. Even adding descants and complex arrangements to a hymn doesn't alter the basic hymn structure; it merely decorates it.

In contrast, the congregation's musical role in Praise & Worship makes no sense without the worship team's accompaniment—the accompaniment is the musical bed upon which the melody lies. It also provides a rhythmic grid that is essential for the syncopations and downbeat rests that are a natural part of the pop melodic style. Without this grid the congregational melody would float aimlessly. Of course, there are exceptions to every musical rule, and not all hymns and praise songs fall neatly into this one. For example, the hymn "For All the Saints" (Sine Nomine) features a unison melody (rather than a four-part vocal structure) that requires accompaniment. In contrast, Melody Green's "There Is a Redeemer" is a praise song that can easily be sung in four parts a cappella.

The Praise Pyramid

One way to understand the melodic, chordal, and rhythmic structure of Praise & Worship is as a pyramid (see illustration below). The voice of the congregation is always most important in congregational song, and Praise & Worship is no exception. However, in Praise & Worship the melody can't support itself, so it must rest on a musical foundation, the chordal and rhythmic accompaniment. Chordal instruments such as piano and guitar provide a harmonic setting for the melody, and to some degree the harmonic movement also provides a basic rhythmic structure as well. Therefore, the chordal layer of the accompaniment is usually a sufficient support structure for the melody, as can be seen in the prevalence of modern worship that succeeds with a simple guitar accompaniment.

The Praise Pyramid

Winds, Strings, Harmonies, etc.

VOICE

Chords (Piano and/or Guitar)

Rhythm (Drums and Bass)

Drums and bass can add a further layer to this support structure, providing further stability to the melody. The bass gives the music feet to stand on, and the drums are like a backbone that adds strength to the whole musical body. Another layer can also be added on top of the voice, chords, and rhythm. This layer of decorative extras can include such elements as vocal harmonies, descants, improvised fills, sustained winds, string lines, and brass hits. None of these are essential to the musical structure, but they do much to enhance it with excitement and unique character.

Vocalists

Before concentrating on the role of the worship team vocalists, we must reaffirm the primacy of the congregation's voice in worship. All that the worship team vocalists (or instrumentalists) do should focus on the goal of supporting confident congregational singing. Therefore, it is instructive to first detail things that undermine the congregation's voice.

Things That Undermine Congregational Singing

Poor repertoire will eventually lead to uninterested worshipers. As I stated earlier, a church's repertoire of songs is their sung theology. If the repertoire is riddled with one-dimensional worship expressions (all celebrative, upbeat songs for example) or shoddy musical materials, worshipers will not invest themselves in the singing.

Unclear instructions will frustrate worshipers. When the lyrics shown in the bulletin are incorrect, verbal and musical cues from the worship team are misleading, and projected lyrics are fumbled consistently, it breaks the trust between leaders and congregation, leading to hesitant participation.

Imprecise vocal entrances by the worship team singers lead to a lag in the congregation's singing. Once again, the worship team's role is to support the congregation's voice. This includes initiating each musical phrase in a way that allows the people in the pews to start together. If the worship team vocalists wait for each other to start singing, they will clip off the first few words of every line, and the congregation will begin still farther behind. This constant game of musical chase does nothing to unite the people in praise.

Worship team vocalists who sing with unique soloistic vocal stylings detract from the congregation's voice. The congregation is a large, cumbersome musical entity that needs deliberate, clear leading. Worship team singers who add the scoops, drops, and other embellishments of their favorite pop stars are overloading the congregation with musical information to which they cannot respond. The vocal leaders' goal should be to sing the basic melody in a rich, even tone that encourages participation.

Overusing harmony can disperse the focus of the congregation's melody. Some worship teams feel obliged to sing in harmony all the time, but this rich vocal texture can create difficulties for those in the pews who are trying to find the melody. It is wise, especially on new or complicated songs, to help the congregation on the melody before introducing harmony.

Uncomfortable vocal range can fatigue the congregation. A comfortable congregational singing range spans from B♭ to D (see illlus. on p. 61), with a possible minor third above and below if prepared well and left quickly. Praise music often requires a transposition up or down, because many published versions of songs are notated based on the vocal abilities of the artist who recorded the song rather than the limited range of the congregation. A further consideration of congregational range is to allow the people to warm up their voices, especially in the morning, by starting the service with songs in a restricted range and then slowly widening to their full range.

Encouraging Congregational Singing

The role of the worship team vocalists is to support confident congregational singing. A number of things encourage this.

The singers should be worshipers. Since the role of the worship team singers is spiritual as well as musical, it is vital that they are chosen for more than their musical skills. Ideally, each singer put in front of the congregation should be an example of a healthy follower of Christ, one who attends church regularly (even when not leading), shows the fruit of a life dedicated to Christ, and has a heart for worship whether up front or in the pew. As I mentioned earlier, the more prominent a musician's leadership role, the more important faith issues become. Singers need not display spiritual rapture every time they lead worship. In fact, leaders often place too much weight on their own ability to lead people in worship—that is the work of the Holy Spirit. However, the singers should be able to guide the congregation through spiritual territory with which they are familiar.

The worship team singers should be musicians. The Psalms encourage us to make a joyful noise, but they also call for us to play skillfully. A worship leader's vibrant walk with Christ must be combined with musical skills.

The singers should have a servant attitude. Effective leadership means giving up one's own will for the sake of the people one serves. For worship team vocalists, this may mean concentrating on the technical requirements of the service and the people's response in worship rather than one's own worship experience. Tom Kraeuter suggests a balance between worshiping and leading: "It is vital that the worship leader actually worship while leading, but if he becomes so completely 'lost in God' that he forgets about the people, then he has missed part of his responsibility. On the other hand, if he is so focused on the people that he misses worshipping the Lord, then he has also missed a major part of his role."[1]

The singers should provide a winsome invitation to worship. Too often worship team singers assume inappropriate roles: cheerleader—energetically (perhaps even maniacally) exhorting the people; disciplinarian—browbeating the people for not participating more fully; or preacher—stopping the service to enlighten the people with a lengthy exegesis of a song or a Scripture verse. None of these are helpful. The worship leader should be more like a gardener; the gardener plants seeds and pulls weeds, but ultimately the real work of growing vegetables is beyond the gardener's control. It is best to assume a pleasant but understated demeanor, maintain eye contact with the members of the congregation, and "conduct" their entrances simply by breathing with them before each line. This provides everything they need without distraction, leaving room for the Holy Spirit to do the rest.

Practical Issues for Vocalists

Let's look at some practical issues for worship team vocalists to lead and work together effectively.

Number of vocalists. The traditional worship team has four to eight vocalists. Ideally they would be distributed evenly between men and women, but in practice there tend to be more women who are interested in singing and more men who play instruments. This large number of vocalists hasn't been heard in pop music since ABBA, the Mamas and the Papas, and Up with People (although it has made somewhat of a comeback in the sound of boy bands like the Backstreet Boys). In the last few years, this distinctive "old school" Praise & Worship vocal sound has given way to a smaller group of singers, usually one lead and one harmony.

While a large group of vocalists is not typical in today's pop music, there are some advantages to this configuration for a group leading worship. Primarily, it helps diffuse the spotlight that is created with one or two vocalists. The fewer singers there are, the more the congregation is aware of their individual traits—vocal quality, emotional delivery, and physical mannerisms—whereas a large group subsumes all the individuals' traits into one moderate entity. In the pop setting it is desirable for the audience to feel a personal connection with the singer, but in the worship setting the people should be connecting with God. The more the congregation is aware of the worship team vocalists, positively or negatively, the less attention they have for God. Another advantage of having multiple vocalists is that it increases options for harmony. Christian worship has a long vocal tradition, and it seems appropriate to maintain a rich vocal sound as one of the unique characteristics of the Praise & Worship sound.

The disadvantage of a large vocal group is that it significantly decreases their agility in leading. The lines of musical communication increase exponentially with the addition of each singer, making it very difficult for the group to act decisively. For this same reason, a barbershop quartet can maintain tight rhythmic control through eye contact and body language, while a choir of fifty people needs a conductor to keep the singers together.

The lead vocalist. When there are more than two vocalists on the worship team, someone must assume the role of "conductor." This lead vocalist is the person to whom the vocalists, instrumentalists, and congregation look for information about tempo, entrances, cutoffs, dynamics, repeats, and modulations. It is not necessary to conduct the whole worship service with full beat patterns, but important moments should be cued in some way. For example, the start of a new verse, especially after a long introduction, should be cued by simply lifting the hand with the palm up in a gesture of readiness a few beats before the cue and then helping the people enter by bringing the hand down like a conductor would cue an entrance. It is helpful for non-conductors to think of the hand as an extension of the breath—the extended hand is simply showing the worship team vocalists and congregation that you are inhaling in preparation for singing the first word. For less difficult entrances, it is sufficient to simply establish eye contact with the other vocalists and then give a slightly exaggerated breath to help them calibrate their entrance.

The lead vocalist can also do quite a bit of leading with just the voice. A simple example of this is verbal instructions such as, "Let's sing it again without the instruments." Often, a spoken cue is given for the repeat of the chorus, simply saying the first few words to let people know to return to that section of the song, or even saying, "Let's repeat the chorus." The problem with these types of verbal cues is that it can be disruptive to shout out instructions at precisely the moment one is trying to maintain flow and extend the mood that has developed. A better solution is to use black gospel style vocal cues in order to provide information without breaking the musical flow. For example, the lead vocalist could cue a modulation by improvising a short melody using the words, "Raise his name even higher." A repeat could be cued by singing the first few words from the section to be repeated or by singing a verbal instruction. Of course, the words and style of the cue will be determined by the style of the song. Improvised vocal cues are difficult to do well, so it is important to practice the skill until it becomes second nature. The leader may need to work out possible vocal cues for an upcoming worship sequence, especially modulations, in order to be prepared.

Using microphones. Vocalists seem to fall into two categories: those who are terrified of the microphone, and those who love it too much. Neither is helpful. Vocalists with an aversion to microphones leave it in the stand and slowly back away, especially if they hear themselves in the monitors. This creates an impossible situation for the soundboard operator, because the singer simply can't be picked up that far away. Those who love mics create a different problem. They spend so much time caressing the mic and striking ecstatic rock star poses that they are distracting. The optimum relationship between the singer and mic lies somewhere in the middle, where the microphone is simply a tool.

We must understand a few technical aspects of the microphone before we can use it effectively. The first is the proximity of the singer to the mic. The closer one gets to the mic, the richer the signal that goes to the soundboard. The farther away the singer moves from the mic, the more background noise is picked up, so the signal going to the board may be only 50 percent singer. The sound operator can turn down a rich signal, but a microphone that is picking up mainly background noise will only add mud to the mix. There is also an issue of phasing that can occur between mics. This problem is best eradicated by following the three-to-one rule: mics must be at least three times as far away from each other as they are from each singer. In other words, if a row of vocal mics is three feet apart, each singer must be within one foot of his or her mic. These issues are solved by having the vocalists maintain an even distance from their mic, usually three to twelve inches. Getting any closer may increase the bass response of the mic, resulting in boominess and pops.

Worship teams must decide whether to hold the mics in hand or keep them in microphone stands. Holding the mics allows for more mobility in general but less agility when turning pages or reading Scripture. It can also allow for a more consistent position between the mic and mouth, especially if the singer frequently turns his or her head. However, holding the mic opens up the possibility of dragging a rock star aura (intentionally or not) into the worship experience. This is a particularly important issue in churches that are experiencing conflict over new worship styles.

Leaving the mics on stands helps neutralize some of the pop overtones and leaves hands free to deal with page turns or conducting gestures. The disadvantage of leaving the mic in the stand is that singers may appear frozen as they try to maintain even proximity to a stationary mic. It can also allow the shy singer to creep farther and farther away from the mic, although this can be combated by placing the mic stand between the singer and his or her music. There is no right or wrong decision, but the worship team leader should understand the issues and be prepared to explain a decision to hold the mics or to keep them in the stand.

An increasingly common microphone option is the wireless headset microphone. On most models, only a thin microphone element can be seen near the singer's cheek. This eliminates the visual clutter of microphone stands and cables, frees the hands, and keeps the mic at a constant distance from the mouth. However, they are not without their drawbacks. Some people find them uncomfortable. Also, any technology with batteries or wireless signal increases the likelihood of problems. If your singers are highly mobile, the wireless headset mic is a good option.

Vocal Harmony

When to Use Harmony

Worship team vocal harmonies can add a wonderfully rich texture to the worship experience. In some respects, vocal harmonies define the Praise & Worship style, but they must be used economically to be effective.

Don't overuse harmonies. When a worship leader has a large group of capable singers in all ranges, the temptation is to let them sing harmony all the time. One should resist this temptation for two reasons. First, a thick vocal harmony from the worship team increases the level of musical complexity for the congregation. While it is good to provide more complex layers of musical participation for the more experienced singers in the pews, it can inhibit novice singers from participating at all. This is especially true of new songs in which people are still trying to master the melody. Second, using vocal harmonies sparingly helps keep the musical textures fresh. Vocal harmonies can be compared to spices—a chef who seasons every dish with salt offers high-sodium monotony; one who uses different combinations of spices for each dish creates an interesting array of tastes that keeps diners surprised and interested.

Tame the harmonizer. As the "cook" of the worship team, the leader must make decisions about where to use harmonies and what type to use. The first step is to tame the "harmonizer." Every worship team has a singer who automatically sings harmony, regardless of the situation; this is often an alto who may want to remain in a comfortable range at all times. Some singers have harmonized for so long that it is nearly impossible for them to sing melody. In any case, the worship team leader must insist that vocal harmonies are not an individual's preference but a decision that is made for the good of the whole team and congregation.

Reinforce song structure. Vocal harmony should be used primarily to reinforce the existing song structure. Harmonies can add excitement to the chorus of a song; they can also highlight particular textual or musical elements in a song. For example, in the chorus of Tim Hughes's "Here I Am to Worship," harmonies could highlight the list of things that the lyrics say the worshiper is there to do: here I am to *worship*, here I am to *bow down*, here I am to *say that You're my God.* This helps accentuate the symmetry of the text as well as its meaning.

Common Types of Vocal Harmony

There are a number of different ways to harmonize worship team vocals. The most common are parallel harmonies that I call the "Tenor Up," "SAT Down," and "Harmony Sandwich." I'll illustrate each of these vocal textures with this short excerpt from Brent Chambers's "Be Exalted, O God."

Tenor Up. In Tenor Up harmonization, the tenor (or soprano if two women are singing) sings one chord tone above the melody to create a ringing harmony as is often done in bluegrass, rock, and folk. Because the tenor is singing a third or fourth above the melody, the line lies in a vocal range that adds a tight, energetic texture to the melody. Simon and Garfunkel are the quintessential example of Tenor Up harmonies. Other examples are rock groups such as the Beatles and Weezer, or with the tenor singing under a female melody as in Alison Krauss and Union Station's "There Is a Reason."

SAT Down. This type of harmonization adds an alto and tenor harmony underneath a soprano melody. This sound is extremely prevalent in black gospel, mass choirs, rhythm and blues, and soul. Not only is it a reflection of Praise & Worship's gospel roots, it also creates an agile, rich vocal texture that thickens the melody without obscuring it. In SAT Down harmony, the alto sings one chord tone below the melody and the tenor sings the chord tone below that. That is, if the melody note is a G over a G chord, the alto sings a D above middle C and the tenor sings a B a third below that. Examples of this harmonization style can be heard in the soul of Aretha Franklin's "Spanish Harlem," "Never Gonna Get It" by modern hip-hop/R&B women's trio En Vogue, Brooklyn Tabernacle Choir's "Hallelu," and just about anything by any mass choir.

Harmony Sandwich. The Harmony Sandwich is identical to the SAT Down harmonization except that it adds the bass vocalist on the melody line one octave below the soprano. This texture doesn't have much precedence in pop music, but it is essential in the worship setting because it gives the worship team bass vocalist a line to sing. It also provides melodic support for both the men and the women in the congregation, while still allowing for harmonic richness.

Harmony Sandwich

How to Create Vocal Harmonies

We will continue by outlining a technique for creating the actual vocal lines for each singer. This discussion assumes some knowledge of chords and basic music theory.

Establish the structural notes. Below (ex. 1) is a short melody with chord symbols, typical of those found in praise song leadsheets.

Example 1 **Melody and Chords**

We will begin by adding a single harmony line in the tenor to create the Tenor Up vocal texture described above. The first step is to sketch the chord tones of the new tenor line. Each of the chord tones in example 2a coincides with a melody note that is at rest on a chord tone. The tenor harmony note is simply the next chord tone above it. The only time the structural note is not on the downbeat in example 2a is in the last measure, due to the suspended C quarter note in the melody.

Example 2a **Tenor Up**; chord tones

"Connect the dots" between the structural notes. Example 2b shows a simple way to complete the harmony line: after adding the next highest chord tone (a third or a fourth) for any melody note that is part of the chord, add a third above any non-chord tone in the melody.

Example 2b **Tenor Up**; filled in, first attempt

As you play and sing through this example, three notes may draw your attention. The first is the D at the beginning of the second measure, which sounds a bit raw without a third in either the melody or harmony. This harmony note could be changed to an F# to sweeten the sound, but because the open fourth is fairly typical of the Tenor Up vocal texture, it is not necessary. In the third measure, the added E in the tenor creates a thicker suspension—actually a one-beat C/G chord. Once again, this is typical of Tenor Up harmonies, and even though it creates a clash between the accompaniment and vocals that would not be allowable in traditional harmonic practice, it is entirely legitimate in this style. The exact opposite is true of the F# in the third beat of measure two. In this case, the D note has been "properly" harmonized with an F# that fits the D chord, but it sounds wrong in this style. This brings up an interesting aspect of gospel and pop harmonies: vocal lines lean toward the pentatonic. That is, the 3rd and 7th of the scale are used sparingly when working in this style. Therefore, the F# in question, while technically correct, makes the music sound "square." This problem can be rectified by changing the F# to its pentatonic substitute, G (ex. 2c). Sing through the line and listen to the difference—it sounds looser and more stylistically accurate.

Example 2c **Tenor Up**; filled in, second attempt

Add a second harmony line. When writing in the SAT Down vocal structure, a similar approach is used.[2] Example 3a shows the alto and tenor on the chord tones below the consonant melody notes. Why was the tenor in measure 2, beat 3, altered to a pentatonic substitute in example 2c, but here it remains an F#? This decision is the result of an important aspect of vocal harmonies: as more voices are added, vertical considerations take precedence over horizontal considerations. In example 2c it was important that the exposed tenor harmony sounded good as its own vocal line, but in example 3a it becomes more important that the tenor line fits comfortably into the chord.

Example 3a **SAT Down**; chord tones

Harmonizing non-chordal melody notes. There are two approaches to filling in harmonies over non-harmonic melody notes (those that don't fit into the accompanying chord). The first is a chordal approach that fills in either a I, IV, or V chord underneath the non-harmonic melody note. Example 3b shows a D chord underneath an A melody note in the fourth beat of the first measure, and a C chord underneath a C note in the second and third measure. There is technically a clash between the accompaniment chord and the vocal chord, but because it is only a momentary shift to a chord within the key, it is entirely acceptable. Also note that the C vocal harmony over a D chord is a common chordal substitution in gospel and pop, often called the IV/V dominant.

Example 3b **SAT Down**; chordal

The second method of filling in harmonies under non-harmonic melody notes takes a more linear approach. The harmonies move in close parallel to the melody, and each line follows the pentatonic rather than the major scale. Sing through the alto and tenor lines in example 3c and hear the pleasing melodic contour that was absent from example 3b, especially in measure 1. Also notice the loose gospel feel that this harmony style provides. Neither of these is a preferred method of harmonization, but both should be utilized when creating harmonies. Above all, use these harmonizing methods only as guidelines, letting the ear be the final judge.

These basic vocal writing techniques will be valid for 95 percent of the situations a worship leader will encounter in the Praise & Worship genre. You can apply the same skills to writing harmonies for brass, strings, and woodwinds. In the rare case that the music style moves beyond what these techniques cover, consult a good jazz or classical arranging book.

Infrequently Used Harmonic Textures

While Tenor Up, SAT Down, and the Harmony Sandwich are the most typical vocal textures in Praise & Worship, there are a number of other variations.

SATB. A four-part texture utilizing soprano, alto, tenor, and bass in their traditional choral roles may be used in Praise & Worship. However, the addition of the bass line in this configuration makes the texture too thick and cumbersome to work well with the standard worship team. The Harmony Sandwich is better for four-part vocal writing because it keeps the basses in a higher, more agile range. At times that call for a cappella singing or full choir, however, the SATB structure can provide an exciting vocal moment. This vocal harmonization is created by writing an SAT Down harmony in the top three voice parts, then simply adding a bass line that follows the bass line indicated in the leadsheet.

SSA. When working with all female praise singers, use an SSA structure. The same SAT Down techniques are used to write the vocal lines, but in order to keep the singers in their best ranges the voice parts must be redistributed. Starting with the original SAT Down lines, in the SSA texture the soprano 2 sings the melody, the alto sings the alto, and soprano 1 sings the tenor line an octave up. Because the melody is surrounded by harmonies it is best to have two singers on soprano 2.

TTBB. An all male vocal ensemble uses the TTBB structure, which is identical to the SSA except that it is sung in the men's range (an octave down from the women) and adds a bass line like the one used in the SATB harmonization. To avoid a dull timbre in this configuration, transpose the music up a step if possible.

Special effects. A number of special effects can be used occasionally as vocal "spices" (like spices, they shouldn't be overused). Sustaining notes on "ooh" can add a soft, rich layer of sound that is appropriate behind a vocal solo. Singing on "aah" produces a full, vibrant texture that can substitute for strings. Descants can enhance praise songs just as they can hymns when the congregation is secure in singing its melody. An adventurous vocal team can take over instrumental roles similar to Take 6's signature sound. Only attempt this if you have a skilled "drummer" and "bassist." An unusual way of harmonizing heard periodically in black gospel or in rock songs such as "The Time Warp" is to place a soprano on a pedal point[3] or static harmony at the very top of their range. This puts an edge on the vocal sound that can cut through the fabric of the music, providing an exciting climax. Last, the spoken word can add an interesting timbre to the vocal ensemble. Robert Shaw was known to have half the choir sing and half the choir whisper the text during particularly quiet passages. Examples of speech-singing from pop music include Aerosmith's "Walk This Way" and the Beatles' "Get Back," which have one or two singers speaking the text of the chorus while others sing it.

Mastering the ability to create all of these vocal harmonies may seem like an unnecessary chore; after all, most singers on worship teams can make up their own harmonies. However, there will always be situations—working with a full choir, for instance—in which the leader will have to create harmonies for the singers. Be prepared to answer questions about when to sing harmony or when the singers' improvised harmonies are not effective.

Guitar

The guitar is one of the most frequently used instruments in modern worship, but it is the least understood by those who don't play it. Perhaps it is confusing to non-guitarists because the physical attributes of the instrument—six unevenly tuned strings—are so unlike the piano or other instruments that have a more or less even choice of notes from the bottom to the top of their range. It behooves the non-guitarist worship leader to learn as much as possible about the guitar, perhaps even learning to play it a bit, because many decisions that the worship leader makes will (or should) be made with the peculiar needs of the guitarist in mind.

Acoustic Steel String Guitar

Range and tuning. The practical range of the instrument runs from the low open E string to an octave above the high E string, although guitar solos often run up to an octave above that. However, the standard tuning of the guitar's six strings—E, A, D, G, B, E, from low to high—is much more important to the guitar's unique sound than its actual range. This configuration of fourths and one third allows the player to press a combination of notes to create chords.

Open chords. Two basic types of chords are played on the guitar: open and barre.[4] Open chords are those that allow some of the open strings to ring when all six strings are strummed. Because the steel string guitar—the typical acoustic guitar used in a worship team—requires so much force to fret, open chords are the easiest to play. In fact, there are many beginning guitarists who can only play open chords.

Barre chords. Barre chords require more strength and skill, because the guitarist uses the index finger as a "bar" across the neck and then configures the rest of the chord with the remaining, weaker fingers. Jazz and rock guitarists use barre chords extensively, but both play the electric guitar, which requires significantly less left-hand pressure to play. On the steel string acoustic guitar, constant barre chording can be fatiguing. Further, the lack of open strings in barre chords creates a bit duller sound with less sustain.

The capo. I once attended a workshop in which a prominent worship leader—a violist—suggested that guitarists should be expected to play in all keys just like any other instrument. This kind of purist attitude is fine in theory, but the practical reality is that string instruments sound best when open strings are used to their advantage. After all, Bach didn't write his thorniest violin partitas in the key of G♭! While guitarists should certainly be expected to know how to play barre chords, it would be cruel to expect them to play a whole worship service in difficult keys such as D♭ or E♭. Furthermore, the resulting sound would be inferior because it wouldn't take advantage of the guitar's characteristic open string ring.

The guitarist solves this dilemma by using a capo. A capo is a springed device that snaps onto the fret board, raising the pitch of the open strings. For instance, a capo attached to the second fret (each fret is a half step) would raise the open strings of the instrument by a whole step. This means that the guitarist can easily play in the key of E♭ by attaching the capo to the first fret and playing the song with D chord formations.

The practical implication of this is that praise sets should generally favor guitar-friendly keys such as E, Em, G, A, Am, C, and D. Using difficult keys is fine as long as a leadsheet with transposed chords is provided for the guitarist using a capo. Also, when modulating, the guitarist may need time to put the capo on or take it off the neck of the guitar. This can usually be done in a matter of seconds, but the guitarist should not be expected to move smoothly from one song to the next while adjusting the capo.

Strumming. The guitarist's right hand produces the instrument's sound using two basic techniques: strumming or picking. With strumming, the sound is produced by quickly dragging a plectrum[5] across the strings. Usually this motion is continued in a pattern of down and up strokes that correspond with the rhythm of the song's eighth- or sixteenth-note pulse, producing the guitar's characteristic "washboard" strum sound. This strumming pattern can be as simple as the "campfire" pattern heard on slow folk songs such as "Kum Ba Yah," or as complex and funky as the introduction to the Doobie Brothers' "Without Love." A skilled player can bring out intricate rhythms within the basic down and up pattern using a combination of stronger and weaker strums, dampening chords with the left hand, and "raking" (a slow, hard strum heard in the flamenco style).

Picking. Picking is a more advanced technique that can be done either with the fingers (called fingerpicking) or with a pick (flat-picking). Either technique produces a harp-like sound that functions similarly to piano arpeggiations. Fingerpicking can be especially useful in ballads where the gentle arpeggiations establish both tempo and harmony. Flat-picking can simply be another way of producing fingerpicked patterns, or it can be combined with aspects of strumming. It is common for the flat-picker to hit a bass note on the downbeat, pick an arpeggiated chord, and hit a chord on the backbeat. Some will even throw little soloistic fills into the pattern or add notes to the bass pattern. There are endless possibilities for both fingerpicking and flat-picking. The worship leader need not decide which technique guitarists will use—they will have their own preferences and abilities. However, be aware of the options and work with the guitarist to find patterns that fit with the music.

Alternate tunings. Advanced players sometimes use alternate tunings that maximize the number of open strings in a given key. Some popular configurations are "Drop D" (DADGBE) and DADGAD. These tunings can be combined with a capo or even multiple capos. Decisions about advanced techniques such as this are typically left to the guitarist.

Electric Guitar

While the bread and butter of worship-team guitar playing is the strummed or picked steel string acoustic, electric guitars are often added to the ensemble. Though the electric guitar is configured the same way as an acoustic, it should be thought of as a different instrument that can make its own unique contribution to the sound of the team. The electric is less effective than its acoustic counterpart when strummed and should instead be used for more characteristic techniques: power chords, riffs, fills, and leads.

Power chords. Previously the domain of heavy metal, power chords are low chords consisting of the root, fifth, and octave (alternative rock bands favor a ninth on top) that give a distinctive crunch to the chord. Made famous in songs such as "Smoke on the Water" and "Iron Man," power chords are often used in a worship team setting to give an edge to a song's harmonic rhythm or to add texture to a sustained chord.

Riffs. Riffs can include anything from the repeated guitar hook in the Beatles' "Taxman" or U2's "Sunday, Bloody Sunday," to the single, damped note that is repeated as rhythm in Fleetwood Mac's "One Wing Dove." Riffs can be extremely useful in a worship team setting because they add texture and rhythmic intensity to the overall sound.

Fills. Fills are short, improvised solo passages typically thrown in between melodic phrases. These can be added at the electric guitarist's discretion and if played tastefully will keep a song's energy going when the congregation is not singing.

Leads. Improvised like fills, leads are solos that are played over the whole form of the song. Solos like those found in pop music are rare in a worship setting, because they displace the congregation's voice for a significant period of time. However, they can be extremely effective as introductions and transitions.

The electric guitar invariably uses some type of sound processing. These sound alterations, called effects, can come from effects boxes (often called "stomp boxes" because they are turned on and off with the foot), digital effects processors, or the guitar amplifier. The sounds chosen for each electric guitar line are almost as important as the line itself, because the effects determine how well the guitar will fit into the overall ensemble. For instance, heavy metal distortion will sound out of place if there is no drummer. A chorus, delay, or reverb effect that can be used to soften the edge of the guitar sound in some settings can end up adding midrange mush in other settings. The worship leader doesn't need to be able to recommend specific effect settings ("How about a stereo chorus with a light tube distortion right there?"), but he or she should be able to provide descriptions of the desired sound ("Could you do something jangly like the beginning of U2's 'Where the Streets have No Name'?").

Synchronizing Guitars

The guitarists should lock in with each other and with the rest of the ensemble. If two acoustic guitarists are playing together (not typically recommended) or an acoustic and electric are both utilized, they need to be perfectly synchronized with each other—not only strumming the same pattern in the same tempo but also feeling the same rhythmic subdivisions. If only one guitarist is playing, he or she should lock into the rhythm of the rest of the ensemble, especially the high hat of the drum set. In the absence of a drummer, the guitarist establishes the rhythmic character of the song. Therefore, it is important to find a guitarist who can appropriately match strumming or fingerpicking patterns to the inner rhythms of each song.

Further Listening

To glean ideas of how the guitar is used in pop music, there are a number of examples to study. Folk singers and modern singer/songwriters will show the numerous strumming and fingerpicking patterns used by guitarists. Modern country music is known for its distinctive Nashville guitar sound. Disco and R&B provide useful examples of the way an electric guitar can add rhythm to a song. Alternative rock bands such as Weezer and Juliana Theory show how thick distortion can be used without sounding harsh.

Piano

The piano is unique among the worship team instruments in its ability to play melody, bass, and harmony simultaneously, as well as virtually any conceivable inversion or voicing. It also has an unprecedented seven-octave range that spans from below the lowest notes of the electric bass to well above the highest soprano. This combination of agility and range has rightly earned the piano its reputation as "the orchestra under the fingertips."

Differences between Solo and Band Piano Playing

The ability to play any way and anywhere one desires often leads to problems when the pianist plays in a band setting. Pianists are accustomed to playing everything all the time as a soloist or accompanist, and they continue to do so with the worship team. However, pianists must adapt their technique to accommodate a band.

The primary change the pianist makes when playing with a rhythm section is to play less. Unlike accompanying a choir or soloist, in a band there is a bassist to lay the harmonic foundation, guitar and drums to keep the rhythm going, and vocalists to cover the melody. This may be nerve-wracking for the pianist at first, but eventually it becomes freeing to understand that one must only supply part rather than all of the accompaniment.

Reducing the use of left-hand octaves. One of the first places the pianist should trim is the use of octaves in the left hand. A solo piano needs the harmonic strength the left-hand octaves provide, but in a band setting this will invariably conflict with the bassist. Hopefully the pianist will adapt his or her technique by hearing the problem or having it pointed out by the worship leader (or a disgruntled bassist). If the technique is too ingrained, some pianists find that they can break the habit by continuing to form their left hand into an "octave hook" but only playing the upper octave (the note under the thumb). This will thin the sound in the low range and solve problems for the band. If the pianist is simply unable to break the habit of playing octaves in the bass, he or she may need to take drastic measures such as covering the lower octaves of the piano or using a sixty-one-note keyboard.

Expanding the use of the piano's high range. While the pianist must trim the use of the bass range when playing in a worship team, the high end of the instrument may be used to great effect. In fact, there are so many instruments in the midrange—acoustic and electric guitar, vocal melody, horns—that the piano is often redundant in this range. The piano can provide an exciting clarity to the instrumental texture of the worship team by playing in the upper register.

Variety. Of course, overplaying in the upper register is no more interesting than overplaying in any other register, which points out the key to creative piano playing in a band setting: listening! Rather than playing in a particular style or range all the time, the pianist should approach the instrument as if it were an orchestra—at times playing a thundering chord like timpani and brass, a bright fanfare like the trumpets, or a placid arpeggio like harp and strings. As one of my composition teachers used to say, "Compositions are like buildings—they need doors and windows." The same is true of piano playing in the worship team; play sparsely rather than in a constant wall of sound.

Resources for learning pop piano technique. Often the worship leader deals with a much more basic problem when it comes to pianists—many can only play written piano arrangements. The ability to "chord" is essential for a worship team pianist, and the worship leader must either audition a person for this skill or be prepared to help the pianist learn it. Some resources include:

- Ed Kerr's instructional video *Keyboards in Contemporary Praise and Worship* (www.kerrtunes.com)
- *The Pop Piano Book* by Mark Harrison (www.harrisonmusic .com)
- *Keyboard Wisdom* by Steven Goomas (www.stevgoomas.com)
- Barry Liesch's keyboard materials at www.worshipinfo.com

Common Piano Textures

A worship leader can communicate with the pianist and suggest basic piano styles for particular songs.

Pop arpeggio. The most commonly used (perhaps overused) piano texture for ballads is the basic pop arpeggio. There are hundreds of variations on this technique, but it typically includes a bass note on the downbeat, melody in the right hand, and a broken chord filled in with a combination of the left and right hands. This is especially useful when only the piano is playing, because it provides a complete accompaniment of bass, chords, and melody. It is less effective when a guitar is fingerpicking because the arpeggios tend to conflict with each other.

Hymn voicing. Four-part hymn voicing can be applied to praise songs as well. The focus here is on smooth voice leading within a somewhat limited range, with the option of using arpeggios or repeated rhythms to fill in longer notes in the melody. This texture is an excellent way to complement a ballad when a guitar is providing rhythmic accompaniment. However, it doesn't have enough rhythmic or tonal energy to stand on its own for too long.

Right-hand clump. Another common texture, which I call the "right-hand clump," sounds just like its name implies. A three- or four-note chord is formed under the melody note in the right hand. When the melody moves quickly or has many non-harmonic tones, the pianist can simply play the melody without losing the general effect. This moving block harmony doubles the vocal melody and harmony and is a good way to provide harmonic support without filling up a lot of space. Often a bass line of octaves, fifths, or a repeated rhythm is played in the left hand.

Two-hand clump. In this texture, both hands play the same blocked chords that were used in the right-hand clump, adding a higher octave to the right-hand clump. Because this expands the range of the line, it adds a wonderfully bright punch to the texture of the worship team. Besides doubling the melody, it can also be used to add brilliance to power chords or brass hits. Obviously, it also eliminates the possibility of providing a bass line.

Upper register. Moving the piano into the extreme upper register is the musical equivalent of opening a window in a stuffy room and letting in a cool breeze. It can be used like the glockenspiel in an orchestra by doubling melodies or highlighting chords, or it can sound like a harp with quiet ostinato patterns that float above the rest of the arrangement. Though the upper register of the instrument is often used for arpeggiated flourishes by performers such as Liberace or Dino, that type of flashy piano technique is rarely appropriate in the Praise & Worship style.

Rhythmic figures. One final texture that is heard frequently in pop piano playing is rhythmic figures. These figures can be as simple as the repeated quarter-note chords of a Coldplay song or as intricate as the piano motive that punctuates Vanessa Carlton's hit "A Thousand Miles." As a jazz orchestration teacher once told me, "Don't forget that the piano is a percussion instrument; feel free to use it that way."

Further listening. Classic pop pianists such as Elton John, Billy Joel, Warren Zevon, and Keith Green are good examples of how the piano typically interacts with the band and voice in pop music. Bruce Hornsby, Vanessa Carlton, and Tori Amos show the piano in a more contemporary pop context. Ben Folds Five and Joe Jackson use a more aggressive style that often takes over some of the guitar's role. Gospel, country, salsa, and jazz should all be studied for their unique piano styles.

Bass

Though the bass seems like a background instrument, it can actually make or break the sound of the worship team. This unsung hero lays a foundation of tempo and rhythmic style upon which the rest of the team builds—if the bass is not in the groove, neither is the rest of the team. So much musical responsibility rests on the bass player because music is understood from low to high. If a note is out of tune or a rhythm is out of time at the bottom of the musical mix, nothing above it will sound quite right.

Introduction

Range and tuning. Most basses have four strings (low to high: E, A, D, G, like the four lowest strings of the guitar), but many newer basses come in five-string models that add a low B and six-string models that also add a high C. This extends the instrument's range but doesn't change the way the instrument is played or the way it fits into the worship team's sound. The bass uses the bass clef and sounds an octave lower than written, so it can produce sound that is felt in the belly more than is heard with the ears. Of course, the amount of sound that one feels rather than hears depends on the way the bass amplifier is adjusted. If a large amp (at least one fifteen-inch speaker) is used, the low end of the instrument can be faithfully reproduced at levels that rattle windows. However, this is rarely appropriate in a church setting, and the bassist will either use a smaller amp (typically with a twelve-inch speaker) or will adjust the settings of the amp to minimize the amount of the lower range that is amplified.

Other types of basses. Though the four- and five-string fretted electric basses are the most common types of basses used in worship teams, there are other types of basses that may be used. The fretless bass guitar is most often used in jazz fusion and jazz-influenced pop. Because it lacks frets, it has a fluidity of pitch that gives it a very human quality. Its tone has a distinct, round buzz made famous by Jaco Pastorious, which gives it more of a "wood" sound than the fretted electric. The string bass (also called the double bass, contrabass, and stand-up bass) is typically used in classical and jazz. Though it is used less often for rock, it provides a warm thump that can drive a song's rhythm. It was used frequently in early rock and roll and enjoyed a resurgence of popularity recently with the Stray Cats and other rockabilly and roots rock groups. It also can be played with a bow, which can lend a beautiful, cello-like quality to ballads, especially in its upper range. The main problem that a worship leader will experience when using the string bass is amplifying its boomy low end in a way that mixes well with the rest of the band.

The bass's harmonic function. Regardless of the type of bass used, the musical function is similar: to lay a harmonic and rhythmic foundation for the rest of the band. Harmonically this means that the bass is normally playing the lowest note of the chord, whether the root or the written inversion. This is not to say that the bassist should only play that note. There is plenty of room for interesting bass lines, but they should not be created at the expense of the primary bass notes.

Rhythmically, the bassist lays a foundation in tandem with the drummer, specifically synchronizing with the drummer's kick (bass) drum. The foundational rhythms established by the bass and the kick drum establish the song's groove and provide a rhythmic grid within which all the other musicians play. Pay careful attention to how well the bass and kick drum lock together. Their playing conflicting rhythms or feeling the rhythm differently will cause a host of problems for the rest of the band. When there is no drummer, the bassist takes over the primary role of establishing the musical foundation.

Playing Technique

Picks. The bassist normally plays by plucking the string with the index and middle fingers of the right hand in alternation, producing a round, robust tone. However, there are other techniques that are useful. Picks are effective in songs that call for repeated eighth or sixteenth notes, especially when the string is damped slightly with the heel of the right hand. The sound can range from thin and metallic to a dry staccato. It was used extensively in the 80s by new-wave bands such as the Cars and is still used by many punk bass players.

Popping and snapping. A bright, percussive sound is produced by popping the string against the fretboard with the thumb and then rebounding with a snap of the string against the fretboard by pulling it with the index finger. This aggressive technique, made famous by Victor Wooten, produces much more volume than plucking, so it should be used with care in the church setting. However, it is entirely appropriate for funk and gospel styles such as Israel and New Breed and can be heard on many disco, R&B, hip-hop, and mass choir recordings.

Harmonics. Bell-like tones are produced by lightly touching the string at a node with the left hand while plucking with the right. The nodes of the string are places at which the string can be evenly divided (half, third, etc.) and that correspond to the notes of the harmonic series above the string. For example, above the G string, harmonics can be played at the G an octave above the open string as well as D, G, B, D (and higher) above that. This complicated bass technique is used primarily in a solo setting. It is more important for the worship leader to be aware that the technique exists and to know that an advanced player may use it in keys such as G, E minor, and D than to understand the exact technique involved.

Pedal points. A musical device frequently used by bassists, especially when playing ballads, is the use of pedal points. The bass could play a C while the chords above move from C to F, G, and back to C. The C bass note dissonates against the G chord, but it is not an offensive dissonance. In fact, it can create an ethereal, mesmerizing sound that can contribute to a meditative atmosphere. In pop music the pedal point is usually played rhythmically rather than as a long sustained note. One common pedal point rhythm is the dotted-quarter, eighth, half note rhythm that frequently accompanies pop ballads. A variation on the pedal point is the use of an ostinato, or repeated motive, rather than a repeated note. The ostinato functions similarly to the pedal point in that it moves in and out of consonance as chords change over it.

Troubleshooting

Eventually, every worship leader will have one of those rehearsals when the band simply doesn't gel but there is no obvious reason for the problem. In these cases, it is often the bassist who is the culprit. This is not because bassists are inferior musicians; it is simply a matter of the bass's role in the overall sound of the band. The bass is responsible to a great degree for setting the tempo and groove of each song, but a difference of a fraction of a second can completely change the rhythmic character. As the saying goes, "There's a fine line between a groove and a rut."

Hearing the beat's subdivisions. Most often the problem is that the bassist fails to hear the subdivisions of the beat the same way the rest of the band does. For example, songs with swing eighth or sixteenth notes imply a totally different rhythmic grid and should color everything the bassist plays. If the bassist doesn't adapt his or her playing style, you may need to stop the rehearsal and make it clear to the players how they should subdivide the beat. A beginning bassist may benefit from putting the instrument down and clapping or singing the rhythm, because it is often insufficient or lazy technique that gets in the way of precise rhythmic playing.

Avoiding conflict with other instruments. Another frequently encountered problem is conflict between the bass, piano left hand, and kick drum, all three of which play in the same range. While the bass and kick drum mustn't be slavishly identical, they do need to reinforce each other's basic rhythms. Anything less destroys the rhythmic foundation of the song. The bassist and pianist should be sensitive to each other's playing to avoid mush in the low range. As I said previously, double octaves in the pianist's left hand are ordinarily inappropriate in a band context. Likewise, a bassist who insists on playing in the tenor range of the instrument conflicts with the piano and fails to fill the bass's important role of providing harmonic foundation.

Playing characteristic, economical bass lines. Many times, worship team bassists are "converted" guitarists. It is sensible to train a guitarist to play bass because the tuning of the instruments is similar and there is often a glut of guitarists. However, these ex-guitarists often produce uncharacteristic bass lines that don't contribute to the band's sound as much as they could. Rather than the melodic approach of the lead guitarist or the constant rhythm of the acoustic guitarist, the bassist provides sparse lines that stay close to the chord roots. Once this basic harmonic and rhythmic foundation is established, the bass is free to embellish with fills and flourishes in between structural notes. Every bass player would do well to concentrate on playing in a lean, muscular style. Satisfying, groove-filled playing is characterized most by what the bassist *doesn't* play.

Drums

The drum set (also called the drums, trap set, or set) is often a mystery to worship leaders who don't play it. Any band leader should learn how to play the drum set—your appreciation for your drummer's skills will grow, you will be able to communicate more easily with the drummer, and you will gain insight into building a song's rhythmic character. However, at the very least, the worship leader should understand the parts of the drum set, how it is played, and how it fits into the musical fabric of the worship team.

Anatomy of the Drum Set

When the drummer sits on the drum throne (stool A), what does he or she see?

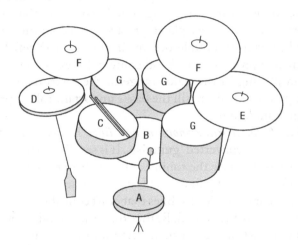

Bass drum (B). Often called a kick drum, the bass drum rests on the floor and is played with the right foot.

Snare drum (C). The snare is normally positioned directly in front of the drummer between the knees; it has metal wires on the bottom head of the drum that buzz when the top of the drum is struck, creating a crisp sound like paper ripping.

High hat (D). To the left of the snare is the high hat—two cymbals that can be opened and closed like a clamshell with a left foot pedal. The ability to open and close the high hat enables a variety of sounds to be produced when hit with the drumstick: a dry staccato when closed, a messy clang when open, and a sizzle when open and shut quickly.

Ride cymbal (E). Unlike the high hat, all the other cymbals in the drum set consist of only one cymbal. The single ride cymbal, which is usually located on the far right side of the set, produces a clear "ping" that allows eighth or sixteenth notes to be played repeatedly without losing clarity.

Crash cymbals (F). Crash cymbals come in a variety of sizes but are all similar in that their complex overtones produce a splash or crash sound.

Tom toms (G). The toms are semi-pitched drums that produce a clean ring or thud (depending upon their tuning and head types) and fill in the range between the snare and the bass drum. Standard sets have three toms that form a semicircle around the snare, with the highest tom on the left.

The Drum Beat

The primary difficulty in playing or understanding the drums is that they coordinate a number of different rhythmic layers simultaneously. The high hat or the ride is used to keep the pulse, which can be simple quarter notes in a ballad, driving eighth notes in rock and roll, or sixteenth notes with complex inner rhythms in funk. These rhythms, which are played with the right hand, are usually simply repeated notes, but advanced players often play syncopated rhythms. The bass drum and snare combine to create a song's basic rhythmic character, or groove. In its simplest form, the bass drum hits downbeats and the snare backbeats, but they usually outline much more complex, syncopated rhythms. This combination of bass, snare, and either high hat or ride completes the drum beat.

While it is not the place of the worship leader to dictate exact beats for the drummer, it is imperative that he or she can indicate a song's groove, suggest places for fills and hits, and correct rhythmic problems when necessary.

Finding the backbeat. The first step in determining groove is deciding where the backbeat goes. The backbeat, usually played by the snare drum, is the strong beat placed opposite the downbeat. The easiest way to figure out where the backbeat should go is to actually dance the rhythm of the song—stomp or step on the downbeat and clap on the upbeat. The clap is the backbeat. The backbeat is often placed on beats two and four, but in fast country or gospel it can be placed on the "and" of each beat (one-AND two-AND, etc.), and in slow ballads there can be a half-note backbeat placed once per measure on beat three. In some cases the backbeat can be delayed, for instance, placed on beat four. It can even be syncopated, landing just ahead of the beat. The worship leader should be able to communicate a song's basic rhythmic gesture either verbally ("Let's use a slow funk beat with the snare on four") or musically ("Try this rhythm: boom, ba-chick, ba-boom, ba-chick").

Once the groove is established, all the players of the worship team must synchronize their parts of the beat to each other. The bass player locks in to the rhythm of the bass drum, the high hat and acoustic guitar mesh, and any instruments that play the backbeat coordinate with the snare.

Fills. With the basic groove intact, the worship leader can focus on helping the drummer find places for fills and hits that will tighten the groove and propel the music forward. Drum fills, as the name implies, fill in the ends of phrases where heightened rhythmic energy can help propel the music forward into the next phrase. Fills are limited only by the creativity and technique of the player and can consist of anything from a simple eighth note run down the toms to complex syncopations bouncing back and forth between toms, snare, and high hat. It is typical to end the fill with a crash (crash cymbal reinforced with the bass drum) on the downbeat of the measure following the fill. Usually drummers will place fills at the ends of phrases automatically and only need to be told if they are playing too much. However, there are times in a song that call for especially large fills, for instance, to create more energy when pushing from the verse into the chorus or as a signal for the full band's entrance.

Hits. Hits are specific rhythms that break away from the regular drum beat. They can be a rhythm that the whole band plays together in one part of a song or a rhythmic cue that prompts a vocal entrance. Hits help to reinforce the congregation's singing, shape the song into a unique character, and tighten the worship team's sound. The worship leader must communicate to the drummer where the hits should go and give him or her time to practice them with the band. Otherwise a nondescript pattern of beat and fills will go on unabated throughout each song.

Below is an example of a basic drum beat accompanying the song "Be Exalted, O God." Compare it to the previous examples of piano and bass to see how it locks in to the other instruments.

Controlling Drum Volume

The most common problem worship leaders encounter with the drums is that they often overwhelm the rest of the team's playing. Sometimes this is a matter of the drummer playing too loudly or too much, but more often it is simply the acoustics of the room.

One way to reduce the volume of the drum set is to not use it at all, opting instead for congas, bongos, tambourine, shakers, and other percussion instruments that produce far less sound. This is an especially good option for small, mostly acoustic worship teams.

Most leaders will want to keep their drums, in which case an acoustic drum shell may be the ideal solution. The drum shell is a plexiglass wall that surrounds the set, reducing the amount of sound that reaches the congregation, and more important, reducing the amount of drum volume that bleeds into the microphones of other worship team musicians. One can frequently see drum shells employed on live TV shows like *The Late Show with David Letterman* where the sound must be controlled for recording.

Churches unable to afford an acoustic shell for their drum set can reduce some volume by having the drummer use special drum sticks called "Hot Rods" or "Lightning Rods" (dubbed "sissy sticks" by one of my drummers), which are a number of thin dowels wrapped together, rather than one solid stick. This design allows the drummer to play with his or her normal technique, yet produce only half the sound of standard drum sticks. Hot Rods should not be confused with brushes, which produce a fuzzy, metallic attack.

Many churches have opted to use electronic rather than acoustic drums. These digital sets are convincing reproductions of the real thing featuring touch-sensitive trigger pads that are played the same way as their acoustic counterparts. Unlike acoustic drums, the only sound they produce is electronic. Therefore there is no bleed-through to other mics, and the sound operator can adjust the electronic drum volume to match the room. You can even choose from a variety of drum-set sounds, such as jazz, rock, or hip-hop.

Not all drummers are happy about replacing their drum sets with drum samples. They claim that electronic drum sets lack the feel and dynamics of an acoustic drum set and that the sound of the cymbals is especially poor. Some compromise by mixing electronic drums with real cymbals, but many drummers want nothing to do with electronic drums at all. In one of the churches I served, the church's pastor and drummer both happened to be at the same concert one evening at another church. The next day, the pastor gave a glowing report about the electronic drums he had heard. He told me how wonderful it was that he could hear the drums without having to plug his ears and suggested that I consider purchasing an electronic set for our church. Later that day, the drummer told me about the same concert, shaking his head in pity as he mentioned the fact that the drummer had used electronic drums, commenting sympathetically, "He must have felt so . . . emasculated."

Ideally, the drummer should be able to control dynamics without the aid of an acoustic shell, Hot Rods, or electronic drums. Realistically, many drummers have only three dynamics: loud, louder, and loudest. It is up to the worship leader to set up an acoustic environment that won't frustrate the drummer (or other musicians), and then insist that the drummer play sensitively with the rest of the team. Playing sensitively means more than just playing quietly. It also means being alert to volume changes within a song, playing hits accurately and consistently, and responding musically to the other musicians rather than driving through the song as if they didn't matter.

Listen to Top 40 radio to glean ideas about how your drummer can fit into the musical context of your own worship team. Like Praise & Worship, pop music encompasses a broad range of styles, and the drummers tend to be more subdued and sensitive than in rock, where they are often the driving force behind the music. However, there are a number of rock drummers that are well worth a listen such as Stewart Copeland of the Police, Lars Ulrich of Metallica, and Neil Peart of Rush. Finally, jazz is the best place to find drummers who respond to what the rest of the musicians are playing; in big band they cue entrances with hits, and in small jazz combos they join in on the ongoing musical dialogue, volleying phrases back and forth with the other musicians.

Hand Percussion

Using hand percussion is another option for adding rhythmic vitality to the sound of the worship band. Instruments such as shakers (maracas), djembe (a large conga-like drum), conga, bongos, and tambourines can either be added to the sound of the drum set or used alone. These instruments can add a unique ethnic flair to a song's arrangement. They are also a good choice for settings in which a drum set would be overwhelming. You would be amazed at how much energy a simple shaker can bring to a song! Of course, hand percussion can be overplayed just like the drums. I've heard songs completely drowned out by an over-enthusiastic tambourine player or an inexperienced djembe player. It is best to think of hand percussion as spices—use them sparingly.[6]

Brass, Woodwinds, and Strings

Vocals, guitar, piano, bass, and drums form the backbone of the worship team, while brass, woodwinds, and strings can contribute an exciting additional musical layer. This section describes some of the ways these instruments can fit into the worship team context but doesn't go into great detail about the technical abilities of individual instruments. To learn more about the range, tuning, and transposition of each of these instruments, consult an orchestration book such as Kent Kennan and Donald Grantham's *The Technique of Orchestration*, 6th ed. (Englewood Cliffs, NJ: Prentice Hall, 2002).

Single Instruments

A few churches are blessed with large instrumental programs that feature a full or partial orchestra on a weekly basis, but the rest of us must be content with a handful of brass, woodwind, and string players to add to the musical mix. Don't despair! Much can be done with just a few musicians added to the worship team's core players. In fact, a number of interesting musical textures can be created by adding only one instrument to the worship team's normal lineup of vocals, guitar, piano, bass, and drums. The added instrument is most effectively a higher-range instrument such as the violin or flute because it expands the tonal range of the worship team without adding mud to the midrange or inverting chords in the bass.

Double the melody line. One of the most common uses of the added instrument is to double the song's melody. Because the music is often readily available, this is easy to do. This efficiently adds a new sonority to the musical fabric, but it becomes monotonous if overused. It is better to use melody doubling selectively—for example, on the song's introduction, chorus, or segues between verses.

Double a harmony line. An added instrument can also double lines besides the melody, such as a vocal harmony. Once again, this has the advantage of readily available music—you can take an existing vocal line from a hymnal or songbook, often the alto or tenor, and have the instrumentalist play it without worrying that it will clash with the vocalists. In doubling either the melody or harmony, brilliance can be added by having the instrumentalist play an octave above the written vocal line—in the case of the flute, this is usually a necessity.

Play sustained notes. Another simple texture an instrumentalist can add to the worship team is a line comprised of sustained notes. Instrumentalists who know some music theory should have no trouble picking one note per chord that will create a logical musical line. If they are not comfortable choosing their own notes, the worship leader can write out a line or circle one note per measure in an existing score. This technique is especially useful for inexperienced players when combined with melody doubling—have the instrumentalist play sustained notes on the verse and double the melody on the chorus for a simple, yet effective arrangement.

Use descants. A more sophisticated use of one instrumentalist added to the worship team is playing descants. Descants, also called obligatos or countermelodies, are musical lines that simultaneously complement the song's melody and have their own interesting melodic contours. There is no formula for writing effective descants, but most descants are soaring melodies in the upper range of the instrument or voice that fill in lulls in the main melody, adding energy and excitement to the song's arrangement. Many ideas can be gleaned from studying existing hymn descants or choral arrangements and then applying them to contemporary styles.

The responsibility for writing descants and other added lines doesn't necessarily rest on the worship leader—many talented instrumentalists will be able to improvise or prepare any of these textures. It is then incumbent on the worship leader only to provide direction about what type of texture should be used in each part of the song and when the instrumentalist should not play at all—for example, "Play the melody on the intro, rest during the first verse, melody on the first chorus, sustained notes during verse two, and descant on the last chorus." Worship leaders should help their musicians grow in the gifts God has given them, so you or another experienced musician must help less experienced church instrumentalists learn the skill of creating their own musical lines when playing with the worship team. I often start out by writing every line that the new musician will play and then slowly let them take over as they become more comfortable. For instance, I'll give them the leadsheet and a piece of manuscript paper with three measures of their line filled in and say, "Here's the music for next week. I've started a sustained line for verse two; see if you can complete it in the same style by next week's rehearsal."

Brass

The brass are by the far the most common instrumental family to be used with the worship team, which is the result of a long history of brass in popular music: big band jazz, Motown, funk, and disco. Unlike the brass quartets and quintets typically used in church, brass sections that are part of a worship team tend to come in groups of three (sometimes two or four) using combinations of trumpet, sax,[7] and trombone. This musically agile group, usually called "the horns," can add anything from organ-like sustained tones to biting percussive accents. They are invariably used homorhythmically; that is, they all play the same rhythms but different notes of the chord. They are usually used to punctuate the rest of the music by joining the rhythm section on a rhythmic hit or providing short motives in the gaps of the melody.

A number of publishers make brass charts available for use with worship teams. Barncharts (www.barncharts.com) and Praisecharts (www.praisecharts.com) offer reasonably priced worship team accompaniments as well as full-fledged jazz/fusion arrangements of hymns and praise songs.

Much can be gleaned by listening to music that uses this style of horn writing. Big band jazz shows horns in highly chromatic harmonizations, as do jazz-influenced music ministries such as Saddleback Church's. Motown, funk, and disco all use sassy, rhythmic horn writing; Tower of Power is legendary for its horns, as are Earth, Wind and Fire, and Blood, Sweat and Tears. The mass choir sound borrows heavily from this style of horn writing as do gospel-influenced modern worship leaders such as Darlene Zschech. Horns have made a comeback in the alternative music world with the return of ska. This upbeat, infectious style (think reggae on caffeine) combines distorted guitars and horns in a unique way and can be heard in such groups as the Mighty Mighty Bosstones, Fishbone, and Christian versions such as the Insyderz and Five Iron Frenzy.

Woodwinds

The woodwinds are rarely used as a family in Praise & Worship or in pop music in general, although they are used effectively by Sufjan Stevens, Supertramp, and They Might Be Giants. It is more typical for individual woodwinds to be used, as described in the "Single Instruments" section, although the flute is periodically used in pop and jazz to put an edge on the horns (think "Shaft"), and of course, the sax is combined with the brass regularly. An example of a larger group of woodwinds playing in modern worship is in the instrumental parts used in the Taizé worship style.

Strings

The string section has some history in pop music, but it hasn't appeared in Praise & Worship to a great degree. Two pop string styles show promise for use in modern worship. The first is the romantic upper string writing popularized by Hollywood that has since made its way to pop ballads of the 50s, soul and R&B of the 60s and 70s, and even funk and disco of the 80s. The string writing in this style is unusual because, unlike traditional symphonic writing, which distributes parts evenly from low to high, the Hollywood pop style eliminates the bass entirely and pushes the rest into their upper registers with little space between the parts. This creates an extremely expressive, even schmaltzy sound that can be layered on top of a rhythm section.

The second approach to pop string writing was made famous in the Beatles' hit "Eleanor Rigby." This approach uses the strings similarly to the way they are used in traditional string writing—in the middle of their ranges and spaced a fifth or sixth apart from each other—but the writing tends to be more rhythmic and biting, especially when the strings are the only accompaniment as they are in "Eleanor Rigby." Beside the Beatles, this style of writing can be heard in Green Day's "Time of Your Life," Elvis Costello and the Brodsky Quartet's collaboration *The Juliet Letters*, and the outrageous rendition of "Purple Haze" by the Kronos Quartet.

Full Orchestra

No unique style of writing for full orchestra has developed in the pop genre as it has for horns or strings, but that is not to say that full orchestra cannot be used in pop. In fact, there are some famous examples of pop musicians teaming up with orchestras, most notably Elton John's "Live in Australia," Metallica and the San Francisco Symphony Orchestra, and much of Mannheim Steamroller's music.

Recently, Keith Getty ("In Christ Alone") recorded a number of his songs with full orchestra.

This type of orchestrated rock and roll is not possible in most churches, but there are some resources for those seeking more rudimentary ways to use their orchestras to accompany Praise & Worship. The most common form this takes is the "orchestrated hymnal." Word Music has released orchestral accompaniments to *The Hymnal for Worship and Celebration* and *The Celebration Hymnal,* the latter of which includes a number of praise songs. Similar arrangements can be found in the orchestrated *Baptist Hymnal* and from www.churchorchestra. com. These somewhat utilitarian arrangements tend to use brass as the core of the sound, which is then doubled in other instruments allowing the arrangements to sound good even when full woodwind or string sections are not available. This creates a sound that is hardly typical of pop, but it is useful for churches who have an orchestra and would like to blend some contemporary music into their worship.

Because full orchestra is not realistic for most churches, it is important to find other ways to use willing instrumentalists. I've found that it can be effective to feature one instrumental section on a particular Sunday. For example, if the choir is singing a song that requires brass quartet, use the trumpets and trombone on the praise music as well. This consolidates the brass players' (and your) time while providing a unique instrumental texture for all the music of that day.

Keyboards

Beyond the acoustic instruments available to the church music ministry are a myriad of sounds that can be created electronically. "Keyboard" is the generic name for any instrument with the familiar black and white keys, but there are a number of different types of keyboards—some intended to reproduce the sounds of acoustic instruments, and some whose sounds are totally new creations.

Digital Piano
Digital pianos are intended to replicate the sound of an acoustic piano as closely as possible. They do this by making thousands of

short recordings (called "samples") of real pianos, which play back when you strike the keys. Higher-end models duplicate the acoustic piano's feel as well, featuring a full eighty-eight-key keyboard with touch sensitivity (it responds to dynamics) and weighted keys (it feels like a real piano's hammer-action rather than a light piece of plastic). In some cases, these digital pianos are incredibly realistic, but like decaf coffee, low-fat ice cream, and diet anything—there's no substitute for the original.

Advantages of the digital piano. So why would you consider buying a digital piano for your worship team? The first reason many churches are using digital pianos is price. An eighty-eight-key, weighted-action digital piano costs as little as two thousand dollars, while a reasonably good acoustic piano starts at ten thousand. Second, the volume of a digital piano can be controlled easily when used with a sound system. Because sound operators have to bring the system up to the volume of the loudest acoustic instrument, bringing down the volume of the piano—the second-loudest instrument next to the drums—will make the sound environment more manageable. This also reduces the stage volume, which eliminates the problem of the piano sound bleeding into all the mics around it. Third, the digital piano offers a wide variety of keyboard sounds, usually including grands, Rhodes, and harpsichord—many also have everything from trumpet to strings—whereas the acoustic piano's sound cannot be altered at all.

Disadvantages of the digital piano. For all the advantages of digital pianos, they can never match the rich sonority of a good acoustic piano. And like all electronic equipment, digital pianos have relatively short lives: the sounds and technology become dated, volume controls and buttons become corroded, and parts are no longer available as new models replace the old. They are like computers—theoretically you could use them forever, but in reality the average user updates every few years. When considering the cost of buying a piano, many churches think that buying a digital piano for five thousand dollars is a wise use of the Lord's money, but in five years they may have to buy another, whereas a quality acoustic piano that receives proper care will last a hundred years or more.

My advice is this: if you plan to do nothing but Praise & Worship with a full band and sound system, a digital keyboard is probably sufficient. If your music ministry includes any acoustic music—choir, vocal solos, music at funerals and weddings—invest in a quality acoustic piano, preferably a grand. Once you have an acoustic piano, you can supplement your sound with a keyboard. When buying a digital piano for a church, I recommend buying an eighty-eight-key, weighted-action keyboard with quality piano sounds and a simple user interface. Most pianists will be happier with a good keyboard feel and fewer bells and whistles. If a larger variety of sounds is needed in the future, you can add a sound module (the brains of the keyboard without the keys) to your existing keyboard.

Organ

Historically, the pipe organ has been the backbone of church music. Called "the King of Instruments" by Mozart, it has incredible tonal variety, volume, and agility. It is the first choice for hymnody, sacred classical literature, and other historic forms of worship. Unfortunately, it has become the pariah of the modern worship movement with seeker churches such as Willow Creek even singling it out as the musical instrument that will dredge up bad childhood church memories in seekers, keeping them from attending church as adults. While the organ cannot be blamed for single-handedly thwarting evangelistic efforts, it certainly finds itself in a new worship context today.

If you minister in a church that has a pipe organ, use it! Too many churches are allowing their pipe organs to fall into disrepair while they shop for synthesizers with organ sounds. The pipe organ, though difficult to blend with pop styles, can still make a valuable contribution to today's worship, especially in the area of hymnody. When available, the organ should lead the hymns because it is so good at encouraging congregational singing. Though not as well-suited to leading in the Praise & Worship style, the organ can nonetheless play some role in assisting the worship team if some adjustments are made to the normal playing style. First, the organist needs to play more sparingly when accompanying praise songs. Unlike leading hymns, in which the organ usually plays all four voice parts using brilliant tones, the organist assisting the worship team should use lighter, higher tones that complement rather than compete with the sound of the band. It may be difficult or even offensive to the organist to adapt to playing in a different context, and it may be frustrating for the worship leader to try to balance the worship team and the organist; however, this musical cooperation reflects a deeper spiritual submission that sends a strong signal to the rest of the church about how the body of Christ can and should function.

The pipe organ is not the only type of organ that exerts a strong influence on modern worship. The Hammond organ, which was introduced to churches in the 60s as an inexpensive alternative to the pipe organ, eventually birthed a completely new keyboard technique that has become the backbone of black gospel. From its beginnings in the African-American church, this flamboyant improvised style, which features scoops, swells, intricate rhythms, and blues scales, has influenced every pop music style. Some examples include Billy Preston's playing on the Beatles' song "Get Back," the jazz organ playing of Joey DeFrancesco, Procul Harum's classic rock hit "A Whiter Shade of Pale," and Caedmon's Call's unique use of the Hammond in an acoustic setting.

Synthesizers

Strictly speaking, a synthesizer differs from other keyboards in that it produces sounds from scratch rather than using digital samples. For our purposes, we will consider a synthesizer any keyboard that produces a wide variety of sounds, unlike the digital piano which is intended specifically as a replacement for an acoustic piano. Rather than boring you with technical details of specific types of synthesis—FM, modular, granular, and so on—I will focus on ways that synthesizers can be used in the context of the worship team.

By far the most common use of the synthesizer in worship is as an electronic version of an acoustic instrument. A synthesized string section can't be an entirely authentic or satisfying replacement for a real string section, but it *functions* similarly to the acoustic instrument it imitates. Because of this, the synthesizer player should do more than choose an appropriate patch (sound) on the synthesizer—he or she must also play like the instrument or instruments that are being imitated. To create the sound of a rich, full string section, don't play octaves in the left hand and a clumped three-note chord in the right; instead, spread the chord voicing out into fifths and sixths as it would be voiced in orchestral string writing. When imitating brass, adapt your playing style to re-create the percussive attack of the brass section; use the volume control or the keyboard's aftertouch (some keyboard models allow the keys to be pressed more or less after the initial attack to affect volume or other parameters) to imitate the sudden dynamic changes that mark the pop brass style. Another effective way of imitating an acoustic instrumental section with a synthesizer is to put one "real" instrument at the top of a chord and have the synthesizer fill out the rest of the chord. Higher sounds tend to color the timbres below them, so if you have one violinist and a synthesizer you can create the illusion of a string orchestra.

Even when you're not directly imitating an acoustic instrument, you may find it helpful to use traditional orchestration as a paradigm. For instance, a generic synth pad will usually complement the overall sound of the worship team if played like an organ, a string section, or a flute trio. Under no circumstances should the synthesizer double the piano part! This undermines the rhythmic clarity of the acoustic piano and adds nothing to the sound of the worship team.

A second and rarer use of the worship team synthesizer is as an entirely new instrument. This can encompass anything from rhythmic programming like the British worship group Grace, using samples like Seattle's Mars Hill Church or creating totally synthesized arrangements like the seminal German group Kraftwerk and the techno genre that followed in their footsteps. However, most churches have a pianist playing the synthesizer rather than a true synth geek with the equipment and technical skills needed for such innovation. Unless your team has a synthesist who can take the lead in this area, you should probably use the synthesizer as a replacement for acoustic instruments.

Using What God Has Given You

I have discussed the many instruments you may encounter in your church, but few people will have all of these at one time. Most of us end up with an odd assortment of musicians of varying abilities. Pray that the Lord will draw excellent musicians to your music ministry, but covenant to utilize and nurture the musicians you have. I have seen exceptional music ministries that have only a hodgepodge of mismatched instruments, yet they discover unique ways of coming together in praise. Perhaps you find yourself with a guitar, trombone, and flute. The guitar can provide the rhythmic and harmonic foundation, the flute can play melodies or descants as described in the section on single instruments, and the trombone can play bass lines or muted harmony lines in its tenor range. Creativity, determination, and prayer will bring solutions to seemingly insurmountable musical difficulties.

Once, an exceptional bassoonist joined my church and volunteered to contribute her skills to the music ministry. I was determined to find a way for her to play, but couldn't figure out how—there was no woodwind quintet for her to join, there is not a lot of sacred solo repertoire for the bassoon, and I really couldn't envision her as a Praise & Worship bassoonist. Eventually I discovered that Mozart's "Laudate Dominum" called for strings and bassoon in its original orchestration. I also found that the bassoon sounded beautiful playing bass lines in Taizé, hymns, and Praise & Worship ballads. I remember watching her play as she was accompanying a song and realizing that this is the way she praises God. Most people use their voices, but for her the bassoon was her praise language. What a blessing to be able to give musicians opportunities to express their hearts to God with all types of praise offerings!

Informing Your Ear

When leading a modern worship team, drawing on a wide range of musical styles, both sacred and secular, is important.[8] If I had to recommend one band that would best train the worship leader's ear, it would be the Beatles. Over their career they explored an incredible range of styles, sonorities, forms, and harmonic languages. Nearly everything being done in pop music today has a precursor in the output of the Beatles.

Another band that provides many lessons for the worship leader's ear is Jars of Clay. Heavily influenced by the Beatles, they are strong songwriters with an innovative use of a wide variety of instruments. The The and Thomas Dolby, though lesser known, both show how acoustic and electronic instruments can be combined in fresh ways.

Cruise the radio dial listening for new styles of music, making mental notes of the things you hear, and then use the ideas. I often introduce a new song at rehearsal and then describe the way I want it to be played by referring to, or even playing, the songs of secular artists who exemplify that style. For example, I've had my teams play Benton Brown's "Lord Reign in Me" in the style of Paul Simon's "You Can Call Me Al," "Salvation Belongs to Our God" with nuances of the Beatles' "A Day in the Life," and "Come, Thou Fount of Every Blessing" with the tip of the hat to Supertramp's "Give a Little Bit." As I see it, you're only as good as the things you steal!

Putting It All Together

The problem with many worship teams is that they play every song exactly the same way. Like a musical meat-grinder, you can throw in any type of musical material in one end, but the same product will come out the other. This type of one-size-fits-all approach gets the job done, but it can become tedious. The worship leader's role is to shape all the individual instruments of the worship team into a coherent whole. The following is an approach to arranging songs for a worship team that starts with song study and ends with instrumentation.

Learn the Song

One of my favorite actors is Anthony Hopkins. In each role he transforms himself into an entirely new character with a unique way of speaking, walking, and interacting. If you were to ask him how he becomes such a different, detailed character in each movie, I would be willing to bet that his answer would be "studying." Detailed study of the script reveals the nuances of the character, which in turn suggests how the actor can create a believable character on screen or on stage.

The problem with most worship teams is that they are more like B-movie character actors. They play every song the same way. The remedy to this problem is to approach each song as a unique expression that requires a unique instrumental arrangement to bring out its inner charm.

Play the song until you know it inside and out. The leader must begin the arrangement process by spending ample time with the song. It is not enough to listen to the song a few times on a CD. Instead, slowly unravel the lyrical and musical meaning of the song by singing through the song a cappella as a prayer, playing the accompaniment at the piano, and trying out harmonies. Ideally, you should memorize the song in the process.

What does the song communicate emotionally? Great song lyrics hone in on one theme and explore it in a fresh new light. What does this song communicate? The agony of the cross? The struggle against sin? The joy of Christian community? Also important are the language and images the author uses to express the theme. Are the lyrics flowery and poetic? Simple and sincere? Light and joyful? Further, the way that the lyrics develop from start to finish is important. Is the theme a bite-sized idea that should be chewed on through repetition? Or is it an idea that develops over multiple verses? The answers to these questions imply very different musical settings.

What is the song's musical content? Songwriters choose musical devices that reinforce the message of the text. They may use a minor melody to convey the poignancy of grief, or syncopation to express the exuberance of a life redeemed. There may be stylistic traits such as lush jazz chords or dance rhythms. Each one of the songwriter's musical choices will suggest different options to the arranger.

What makes the song unique? Ultimately, the worship leader must study and understand the lyrical and musical content—as well as the interaction between the two—and discover what makes the song unique and interesting. Is it a Celtic-inspired melody such as "Jesus, Draw Me Ever Nearer"? An arresting chord change such as the minor V chord in "Amazing Love"? A Latin groove like "Mourning to Dancing"?

Adapt the Music

Understanding the uniqueness of the song shouldn't be a straitjacket; it's a starting point in rendering the song in a way that remains faithful to its unique character while adding the worship team's own unique twist. I compare the process to the way a jeweler works with a diamond: each song is uniquely beautiful, deserving an arrangement that presents its inherent natural beauty in the best light.

Establish the groove and style. Your study of a song will uncover the basic rhythmic character inherent in the melody. This needs to be translated into what is usually called the "groove" in pop music. Some melodies are extremely malleable, taking on virtually any groove that accompanies it. However, some require very specific types of rhythmic accompaniments. For instance, a syncopated melody will require an accompaniment that provides a strong rhythmic structure. If the melody's eighth notes swing, the accompaniment must accommodate that. I usually find it helpful to dance and clap while singing the melody in order to discover a song's groove. (Go ahead, no one's looking . . .)

There are hundreds of music styles to choose from. You don't have to choose a different style for every song, but each song should have a distinctive personality. For example, the melody of "Come, Let Us Worship and Bow Down" is fairly syncopated and features phrases that begin on an upbeat. This, coupled with a simple chord structure, implies a country backbeat to me, so I usually have the drummer use brushes to get a light country sound. Of course, this is only one interpretation of the song's style. I've also heard it played effectively as a ballad and a driving rock song.

The important thing is to avoid shoving a "square peg" song into a "round hole" arrangement. "Holy, Holy, Holy" can be accompanied in a reggae style, but it betrays the theme and the music of the song. However, Brian Doerksen's "I Lift My Eyes Up" works well in that style. You can hear the effectiveness of different arrangements by listening to different recordings of the same song. For example, compare Sonic Flood's or the Insyderz's recordings to the original recordings of "I Lift My Eyes Up."

Experiment with adapting song styles on your own. Try some different styles on Darlene Zschech's "Jesus, Lover of My Soul": first, play it as a gospel ballad the way she originally performed it; next, try it with a driving rock beat; finally, accompany it with an up-tempo country beat with snare on the "and" of every beat. Which is most effective? Do any of these renditions bring out something new and useful in the lyrics or the music? Next, set "Lord, I Lift Your Name on High"—perhaps the most adaptable of all praise songs—to different music styles: punk, country, reggae, salsa. Most of these styles will only remain personal experiments, but perhaps you will find one of these styles influencing the way you approach the song in the future.

Change chords (if needed). Many musicians, especially those trained classically, are enslaved to the page. In pop music, however, the score should be thought of more as a starting point than the final word. The fact is that most pop songwriters create music by ear, and they write a score after the fact. The music on the page is either a transcription of a particular performer's rendition of the song or a simplified piano version of the song that is playable by pianists of all skill levels. Further, in the pop aesthetic, each performer is expected to put their own unique twist on the song.

Since there is no "official" version of the song, the worship leader is free to make tasteful changes, especially to the chords. Many chord charts, especially those that circulate on the Internet, use the lowest common denominator chords of I, IV, and V. Often, a few simple chord changes can create a more exciting song. As with choosing a music style for a song, the chord changes should enhance the song rather than detract from it. If the music style or chord changes draw attention to themselves, they are not ul-

timately serving the song. Instead, seek to make changes that are
at once unique and natural. Also, remember that changing chords
all the time will confuse the congregation and the worship team,
so do it sparingly.

Arrange the Song for the Worship Team

The next step in the process of bringing a song from the page
to the ear is to arrange the song—that is, to give different musical
roles to the various instruments and voices of the worship team. We
will approach this from three different angles: front to back, low to
high, and beginning to end.

The Sound Stage (*front to back*)

When mixing music, recording engineers often talk about the
"sound stage"—the imaginary stage upon which they place recorded
sounds, giving a sense of three-dimensional sound. In movies, sound
placement is quite literal ("make those footsteps move from left to
right"); in audio recording it is more figurative ("bring that vocal
to the front"). A similar process can be applied to the voices and
instruments of the worship team: each occupies a space in the foreground, middleground, or background.

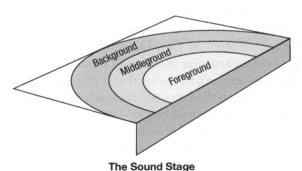

The Sound Stage

Foreground. The term *foreground* can be applied to music in the
same way that it is applied to visual art. It is an object (sound) that
occupies a closer or more prominent place than all other elements,
thereby drawing the attention of the viewer (listener). Because the

worship team's role is to support congregational singing, the foreground is normally occupied by the melody. This doesn't necessarily
mean that the worship team vocalists are the loudest element on
the sound stage. In fact, one approach is to leave a "hole" where
the vocals should be—a hole that the congregational voice fills.
While the praise song's melody usually occupies the foreground,
there are many gaps between melodic phrases that can be filled with
instrumental interjections. However, it is important that multiple
elements don't fight for a place in the foreground at the same moment in the song.

Middleground. The middleground tends to be occupied by the
guitar or piano—the chordal layer of the *Praise Pyramid*. Many worship leaders make the mistake of having both the piano and guitar
play throughout every song, but this tends to lead to ill-defined
arrangements. Instead, assign either the piano or the guitar as the
lead instrument for each song, and delegate the other to a more
supportive role. For instance, on "Lord, I Lift Your Name on High,"
I like the jangly, rhythmic backbone that the guitar can provide,
so the guitar takes the lead while the piano plays more sparsely.
However, on ballads the piano often takes over as the lead instrument while the guitar rests, strums whole notes, or plays some other
background role. The middleground can also be a descant, echo,
instrumental line, or prominent harmony that plays a secondary
role in the arrangement.

Background. The background is filled with instruments and sounds
that provide depth to the arrangement but don't draw attention to
themselves. This can include drums, bass, sustained synthesizer
chords, and background harmonies. Background elements are usually at softer volumes than the foreground and middleground, but
more important, they are less active. This is similar to the visual arts
in which the background elements are softer colors, drawn with
much less detail than foreground elements. This eliminates clutter,
allowing attention to remain on the foreground.

Of course, these delineations are relative. There is no specific point
at which a musical idea moves from middleground to background.
Likewise, there are no mandatory functions for each instrument. The
bass may often be a background instrument, but there are certainly

times that it is appropriate for it to move to the middleground or even the foreground. The important concept to grasp is that a worship team in which all instruments and vocalists play with the same volume and the same intensity at the same time will have a two-dimensional sound. Assigning musicians or musical lines to the foreground, middleground, and background will create three-dimensional depth to each song.

Tonal Placement (low to high)

Just as each musician should have his or her own place from front to back on the sound stage, each one should also occupy a particular place from low to high in the worship team's range. Human hearing spans from 20 Hertz (20Hz) to 20,000 Hertz (20 Kilohertz or 20KHz), yet the standard worship team is focused almost entirely in the middle range. As the chart on page 175 shows, the singers, the guitar, the piano, the upper end of the bass, and much of the drum set all fight for a piece of the midrange real estate, resulting in a thick, muddy sound. Paying attention to issues of range will bring clarity to the worship team's sound.

Give each instrument its own place in the worship team's range. Because so many voices and instruments are vying for the same tonal area, the best way to clarify the team's sound is to pull as many instruments away from the midrange as possible.

Begin by adding bass to the bass. Many bass players favor a bright sound because it cuts through better, but in the end it contributes to the team's overall sound problems. Have the bass player adjust his or her amp settings so that the bass is providing a substantial bottom end. One trick that recording engineers use to get the right bass sound is to take all the low end out of the bass sound, adjusting for the exact *character* of sound the bassist wants using only the midrange and treble controls. Once the desired tonal character is established, bring the low range volume back up. This results in a bass tone that has the character the bassist desires and the substantial low end required to balance the worship team. It is also important that the bassist plays primarily in the bass range. Slapping, chords, and riffs all the way up the neck can be effective, but make sure the

Frequency Ranges of Commonly Used Worship Team Instruments*

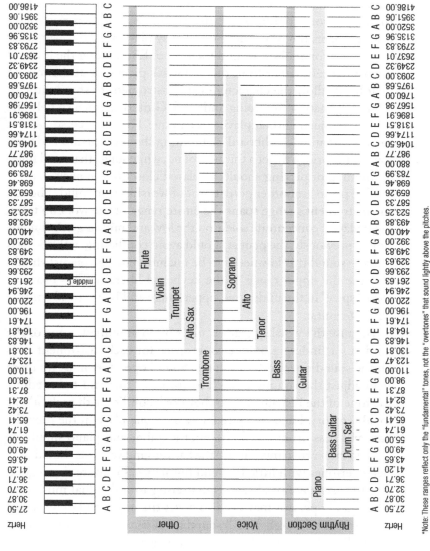

*Note: These ranges reflect only the "fundamental" tones, not the "overtones" that sound lightly above the pitches.

bulk of the bassist's playing provides a foundation for the team's tonal mix.

Next, thin the acoustic guitar sound. Just like the bassist, the guitarist may desire a tonal shape that is at odds with the needs of the whole worship team. Guitarists usually want a deep, rich sound that resonates the way it does when they play solo. However, what is resonant for a soloist is mud for a band. Eliminating the low end almost entirely, either from the guitarist's pickup or at the mixing board, will allow the character of the instrument to shine through while eliminating thumping and mud. Guitarists can also help the sound by adjusting their playing technique. For instance, songs that call for rhythmic "washboard" strumming should be strummed back toward the bridge to get a thinner sound, while songs that need fuller strumming or picking should be played closer to the neck.

The piano is another perpetrator of worship team mud. Though the instrument's range spans the entire range of the worship team, most players concentrate solely on the low and midrange. As I mentioned previously, the pianist should avoid conflicting with the bass range—sound this low needs to be uncluttered. The pianist should also use the upper range of the keyboard liberally. This provides tonal "spice" in the underused upper range and helps avoid conflict with the guitar.

Because the worship team is most often amplified, some of the burden for finding a unique sonic space for each instrument rests on the sound operator's shoulders. Sound operators must do more than adjust the volume of each instrument; they must also adjust the tone of the instruments so they don't conflict with each other's tonal territory. Each occupies its own unique place in the mix: the bass and bass drum should boom, the guitar and piano should be defined rather than muddy, and the background vocalists should have rich overtones with little low-end resonance. Be aware that a good overall mix may not always be flattering to individual musicians. The sound operator may need to boost the upper end of a vocalist to help it cut through. It will sound great in the mix, but perhaps a bit shrill to the singer. This is one of the sacrifices a musician makes for the good of the team.

Use doublings. When the instruments of the worship team play different musical lines in the same range, it leads to an unfocused, muddy texture, but when they double one another in unison or at the octave, it can reinforce important musical ideas and bring clarity to the arrangement. The classic case of doubling occurs between the bass, bass drum, and left hand of the piano. When these elements are playing different rhythms, the resulting chaos throws off the song's groove. When they are doubling the same rhythm and musical line, it creates a rock-solid foundation for the rest of the band. Another common example of doubling is when the guitar and bass play the same riff together, as is heard in the Beatles' "Taxman." The possibilities are endless: electric guitar and saxophone, piano and guitar, flute and trumpet, and so on. Note that the doublings don't have to be exact. There can be slight variations in rhythm as long as the underlying rhythm is the same. Melodic lines can be doubled in thirds or sixths rather than unison or octaves. All these forms of doubling help weave the strands of the worship team into a cohesive and clear pattern.

Vary rhythms. Another way to leave room for each instrument is to use different rhythmic motives in instruments that occupy the same range. For instance, if the piano and guitar both arpeggiate chords in the same range, there will be constant conflict for dominance. A better approach is to have one roll a chord on the downbeat of each measure while the other arpeggiates. If a synthesizer is holding sustained chords in the midrange, the guitar shouldn't fill up the same range with uninterrupted strumming. Instead, sparse picking would be appropriate. The rule of thumb is that when instruments are not doubling each other, they should choose different rhythmic textures from those around them: sparse balances busy, staccato balances legato, large leaps are balanced by sustained or static tones.

ELEMENTS OF TIME *(BEGINNING TO END)*

The descriptions of the sound stage and tonal placement may give the impression that the worship team musicians play very limited roles: the lead vocalist is foreground and the drummer is background; the guitar lies in the midrange and the bass is relegated to low range. This would make for very boring arranging indeed! Praise-song arrangements can be saved from this tedium when the musicians take on different roles—foreground, middleground, background; low, mid, high range—at different times in the arrangement. For instance, the bass player may be playing a low-range, background musical line for much of a song but move an octave higher in one verse of the song or play a short foreground role at some point. The ongoing interplay of musical roles takes place on a large scale—piano is middleground in the verse and guitar is middleground in the chorus—but there are also points in an arrangement in which roles are interrupted only momentarily.

Hits. Nothing is more monotonous than a rhythm section that drones on unabated throughout an entire song. *Hits* are rhythmic interjections that turn the arrangement from a tedious monologue into an exciting musical dialogue. They are most often a foreground rhythm—usually played by the whole band—that is interjected in the spaces left by the foreground melody. For example, in Sonic Flood's rendition of "Open the Eyes of My Heart," after the words "I want to see You. I want to see You," there are two hammered chords before the chorus starts again. The song would certainly not fall apart without this rhythmic nuance, but it lends a burst of energy that fills in the gap between the melody, propelling the arrangement forward.

Hits can also take place underneath the melody, providing momentary relief from the band's ongoing chording with specific full band rhythms. For example, in "Open the Eyes of My Heart" I often bring the arrangement to an apex on the words "As we cry holy, holy, holy" with the whole band hitting the rhythm HO - LY, ho - LY, HO - ly.

Fills. Fills, as the name implies, fill in spaces in the arrangement. The word is most often used to describe drum fills, but any instrument can play a fill. Unlike hits, fills are usually a short improvisation played by one instrument rather than a predetermined rhythm played by the whole group. They are similar to hits in that they provide musical energy precisely where the song sags. For example, in the section of "Open the Eyes of My Heart" after the words "I want to see you," there is a four-beat lull in the melody. Sonic Flood fills this with a rhythmic hit, but it could just as appropriately be done with a fill by an electric guitar or piano. Fills are often added intuitively by instrumentalists (or even vocalists), but if all the musicians pounce to fill the same four-beat rest it can result in momentary anarchy.

Cues. Usually played by the entire band, cues are rhythmic motives intended to signal an upcoming entrance. This is very common in jazz bands where the drummer prepares almost every section's entrances. In praise music, the use of cues is not as frequent, but it can be extremely helpful to the congregation. For example, Graham Kendrick's "Restore, O Lord" ends with a particularly tricky melodic rhythm followed by a rest and a quarter-note pickup into the last phrase. I find that if the band plays a chord the beat before the congregation's last entrance, it cues them as clearly as if a conductor had given them a preparatory beat. In fact, cues are most effective when approached like a conductor—provide a decisive preparatory beat and the congregation will be compelled to enter together.

Breaks. Perhaps it is easiest to think of *breaks* as fills without the fill. That is, the gaps or transitions are filled with silence rather than notes. This is a technique organists have used for years. With the sudden cessation of sound, the congregation is alerted that something is about to change and is thereby cued for their next entrance. In praise music the pauses tend to be relatively long (two to four beats) and prepared and concluded by a hit or fill.

The sound of the worship team is like a block of wood; the tools described above are like chisels with which you can shape the sound. If you don't pay attention to the sound stage, tonal placement, and elements of time on every song, the worship team's leadership becomes a shapeless mass of sound that does little to encourage the congregation's participation.

One of the keys to creating interesting praise-song arrangements is to have a repertoire of techniques gleaned from listening. I recommend listening to pop, Christian, or modern country radio to study how professionals arrange songs. How do they treat foreground, middleground, and background? How do they separate the ranges of the instruments so that they don't conflict? How do they arrange the song with hits, fills, cues, and breaks to keep the song fresh and engaging over time? Another approach is to listen to one of your favorite songs over and over again on headphones, studying every detail of the arrangement—perhaps even mapping out the sound stage, tonal placement, and elements of time. Careful listening will soon turn into creative arranging.

6

Timeless Hymns in a Contemporary Context

T hanks for ruining my favorite hymn," the agitated congregant said as he walked out the doors of the church.

I was moved that the man cared so much about the songs we used in worship but disappointed that he saw hymnody as a static tradition—something to be admired like a butterfly pinned to a board in a display case. I wished I could have explained that the whole history of hymnody is one of adaptation to new contexts, exchange of texts and melodies, and revision according to the tastes and theology of each new hymnal editor. Most of all I wanted to tell him that I was on his side. I have a deep respect for the two thousand years of Christian hymnody that has been lovingly handed down to us, and I will do everything in my power to make sure that I pass it on to the next generation.

A Case for Context

Living traditions, just like living organisms, either adapt to their environment or die. And no one can argue that the environment of worship has not changed dramatically in the last forty years. Since Vatican II and the Jesus movement, new forms of worship and music have become commonplace in worship. In fact, the praise band is replacing the once ubiquitous organ as the main worship leader in many churches.[1] If we care about the great hymns of our faith, we need to find ways of building bridges between old hymns and new worship contexts. One way of achieving this is to create new arrangements of hymns that are appropriate for use by praise bands.

"Sacrilege!" you cry. "That would destroy the very essence of the genre!"

While it is true that many tasteless renditions of hymns have been heard in contemporary worship settings, it need not be the case. I would argue that there are even times when a contemporary setting for a hymn is more stylistically appropriate than what is found in the hymnal. In fact, it's difficult to even talk about "the great hymns of the faith" with any sense of stylistic unity: Do we mean Latin chant? German chorales? Metrical psalms? Watts and Wesley? Gospel hymns? Shape-note singing? Modern writers such as Fred Pratt Green? All these arrive in our hymnals with very different origins, worship contexts, and transmission histories, yet we often think that we provide an equally satisfying modern context for them by singing them in four-part harmony accompanied by the organ. We should explore the many options available to us in order to enliven the congregation's singing and deepen their understanding.

A number of factors speak in favor of the contemporary praise team leading hymns. First, the praise team is the primary worship ensemble in many churches. It would be a shame to close off the riches of past congregational song in order to maintain stylistic purity of historic congregational songs. The fact is that in many churches, hymns will either be led by the praise team or they won't be sung at all. Second, the post–Jesus movement evangelical church is beginning to realize that it didn't invent worship and is attempting to build bridges to its heritage. Contemporary worship practitioners are recognizing that the Praise & Worship genre doesn't address some of the deeper theological issues as well as older hymns do. This has resulted in a slew of modernized hymns.[2]

The results vary, but in general the trend is healthy. Finally, many wonderful hymns have fallen out of use. Reintroducing them via the praise band may give them renewed life with a new generation of worshipers.

However, we must proceed with caution. Many hymn modernizations just sound awkward. If the praise band arrangement isn't done tastefully, it can end up sounding like a hymn version of the "Hooked on Classics" series that matched classical pieces with disco beats. The danger of trying to fit a square peg in a round hole goes beyond aesthetic sensibilities. Many modernizations mangle the hymn melody in the attempt to fit it to a pop beat. This can erode the singing confidence of the congregation. For example, Promise Keepers made famous a rendition of "A Mighty Fortress Is Our God" that forced singers to wait after each phrase while the band completed a four-measure groove. David Crowder's rendition of "All Creatures of Our God and King" jumps between octaves on the "alleluias," which makes for interesting listening but very difficult congregational singing.

The point is that the praise band can lead hymns well, but it is only one of many options: organ, piano, orchestra, or a cappella singing. What follows are suggestions for creating aesthetically satisfying hymn arrangements for the praise band.

Study the Original Hymn's Text

To appropriately recast a hymn, you must first understand the original. A thorough examination of text and music will allow you to discover the inherent beauty of the hymns, much as a jeweler studies the gem to determine a setting that will enhance it.

Poetic Tone

What is the tone of the poetry? Joyful? Wistful? Confident? Pleading? This will be a primary factor in your decisions about a new setting. For example, I have used a country/folk style with a heavy backbeat on "Come, Ye Sinners, Poor and Needy" to bring out the rustic camp-meeting revival quality of the text, while Craig

Curry uses a sweet jazz ballad feel in his choral setting of the same tune, which highlights the tender text of *Cradle Hymn*.

Text Background

Be aware of the historical background of a hymn. Knowing that Horatio Spafford penned the words of "When Peace Like a River" ("It Is Well with My Soul") as his ship passed by the spot where his daughters had recently drowned will (hopefully) guide you away from using a sprightly pop beat for an accompaniment. There are also background considerations of a more local nature: associations for a particular congregation may be too strong if a hymn has just been used at the funeral of a well-loved member, or the hymn itself may be such sacred ground that to tamper with it would feel like a violation of the congregation's trust. During the study of a hymn text, you may also decide to edit the number of verses or revise archaic language. Consulting a hymnal companion or other hymn resource will give you insight into the musical background of the hymn. Discovering that a hymn tune was originally intended to be sung monophonically, comes from a folk tradition, or was written in the popular style of its day can lead to more creative and informed modern interpretations.

Study the Original Hymn's Music

Each song has inherent structural, melodic, and harmonic characteristics that must not be betrayed.

Tempo

One of the pivotal components of hymn tunes is tempo, which is closely related to phrase structure and breathing. Every good melody is comprised of phrases that allow time for both enunciation and breath. A wise worship leader will choose a tempo that is slow enough for the words to be comfortably articulated, yet fast enough that each phrase can be sung in one breath. Tempo is also a major factor in stylistic appropriateness—at a certain point, increasing the tempo of a ballad like "Be Thou My Vision" (Slane) turns it into a waltz!

Range

At its most fundamental level, a hymn's melodic range is the span from its lowest note to its highest. Naturally, it is important to keep a song within a comfortable singing range for the congregation; however, it is even more important to keep songs within a comfortable tessitura. As I stated in chapter 3, tessitura refers to the area where the bulk of the notes in a melody lie, rather than just the extremes of the range. One further element of range is melodic climax, a hymn's unique way of building and releasing melodic energy. For example, "Be Thou My Vision" begins on the tonic and slowly widens its range both up and down, creating a wedge-like climax. "Joy to the World" (Antioch), on the other hand, begins at its highest note, creating a sense of energy that supports the lyrics well. Any new setting of the melody must appropriately reinforce these nuances.

Scale

One is tempted to categorize melodies as happy (major) or sad (minor). This is far too simple, not only because non-tonal scales are frequently used, but also because there are so many shades of emotion captured in hymns.

One of the most commonly used scales, especially in early American hymnody, is the pentatonic scale. The "major" pentatonic scale (C, D, E, G, A) is used in "Amazing Grace" (Amazing Grace) and "Brethren, We Have Met to Worship" (Holy Manna), while the "minor" pentatonic (C, E♭, F, G, B♭) is used in "Come, Ye Sinners, Poor and Needy" (Arise) and others. Both forms of the pentatonic scale lend a folksy, floating quality to the tunes.

Modal scales, or "church modes," were used exclusively in the early church until they gave way to tonality in the Baroque era. Modal melodies tend to feel sturdy, yet lyrical, and much less goal-oriented than tonal melodies. Modal scales include the Dorian (C, D, E♭, F, G, A, B♭, C), which is used in "Built on the Rock the Church Doth Stand" (Kirken Den Er Et), Aeolian (C, D, E♭, F, G, A♭, B♭, C; also called the natural minor scale), heard in "O Come, O Come, Emmanuel" (Veni Emmanuel), Phrygian (C, D♭, E♭, F, G, A♭, B♭, C), such as Luther's "Out of the Depths I Cry to You" (Aus Tiefer Not), and Ionian (C, D, E, F, G, A, B, C)—the same notes as the major scale, yet they behave differently as can be heard in the chant "Of the Father's Love Begotten" (Divinum Mysterium).

Chromatic scales have been used fairly extensively in hymns for the last two hundred years. Actually, true chromatic scales are not used in hymns, but chromatic alterations are. This chromatic material adds a sweetness and romanticism to melodies such as "O Little Town of Bethlehem" (St. Louis).

Melodic Character

Every melody has a unique fingerprint that is due in part to measurable elements such as scale, range, and climax. However, there are much subtler elements at work—rhythmic gestures, intervallic content, music style—that create the spirit of the melody. For example, the repeated melody note of "Peace, Perfect Peace" (Pax Tecum) creates a placid, peaceful spirit. Very different is the rustic energy that results from the quick leaps and runs of "I Sing the Mighty Power of God" (Ellacombe). The marcato rhythms of "Crown Him with Many Crowns" (Diademata) or "Onward, Christian Soldiers" (St. Gertrude) are unlike the legato of "Beneath the Cross of Jesus" (St. Christopher) and the lilting dance rhythms of "Love Lifted Me" (Safety). Each melody has a unique melodic character that suggests a unique arrangement.

Harmonic Implications of the Melody

Analyzing a hymn's existing harmonies before creating a new chord structure for a praise band setting may be helpful, but even more instructive is looking for harmonic implications embedded in the melody. By understanding that folk, pop, and jazz tend to have one chord change per measure whereas hymns mostly have a new chord each beat, we can deduce that arpeggiated melodic segments may necessitate using the outlined chord in any new harmonic setting. For example, the first measure of "Come, Thou Almighty King" (Italian Hymn) outlines the tonic chord, as do measures 7 through 8 and 13. It would be awkward to try to harmonize these measures with anything other than the tonic. It would also be difficult to ignore the harmonic implications of chromatically altered notes such as the raised fourth in measures 6 and 11 of "Crown Him with Many Crowns" (Diademata), which begs a V/V (E in the key of D), or key changes such as the one in "I Heard the Voice of Jesus Say" (Vox Dilecti).

There are many layers in each hymn text and melody—and even more interesting discoveries to be made by observing the interaction between text and melody. Detailed analysis of all these elements contributes to an informed and appropriate praise band setting of the original hymn.

Establish the Groove

Rhythm is the essence of pop music, and pop music is the essence of praise music. Therefore, the first step in transplanting a hymn into the soil of the praise band is to determine the rhythmic "groove." The groove is a pop song's beat, or "rhythmic gestalt," which is determined by the rhythmic interaction of all the musical elements. It is usually summarized by the drum set (see chapter 3). Each genre has characteristic grooves: jazz swings the eighth notes, bluegrass has strong backbeats, and punk is propelled by driving eighth notes in the bass and guitar. The main difference between the groove in a pop song and contemporary congregational song is that the latter must, in the end, support and encourage group singing.

The first step in establishing groove is to determine an approximate tempo. As I stated previously, a hymn's tempo must be slow enough for the words to be comfortably articulated, yet fast enough that each phrase can be sung in one breath. With most hymns this allows for a reasonably wide range of possible tempos. When choosing a tempo for a hymn led by the praise band, remember that "contemporary" is not synonymous with "fast." Many hymn modernizations use such quick tempos that the congregation is left gasping for breath and all the unique aspects of the hymn are neutralized.

Next, find the backbeat. The backbeat, usually played on the snare when a drum set is involved, is the most important factor contributing to a song's unique dance character. For example, marches and polkas have a backbeat on every upbeat (one AND two AND).

Backbeats in rock, jazz, pop, and folk usually occur on beats two and four (one TWO three FOUR). Ballads often have a backbeat only on beat three (one two THREE four), creating a half time feel. The easiest way to find the backbeat when creating a hymn arrangement for a praise band is to stomp and clap along with the melody until you find a backbeat (and groove) that feels right. For example, try stomping and clapping to the tune Holy Manna. Placing the backbeat (clap) on the "and" of every beat would create a polka or upbeat country feel that makes the melody feel choppy. A backbeat only on beat three eliminates the melody's rustic character. To my ear, a backbeat on beats two and four reinforces the inherent rhythmic character of the melody.

Of course, finding the backbeat is only the start. There are endless variations of any groove, which makes the groove exciting or intimidating depending on your outlook. Those who find it intimidating may want to consult a drummer. If you can sing the hymn melody in the desired tempo while stomping and clapping your basic groove, the drummer should be able to interpret that into a more complex and subtle groove. If you have access to a computer program like Apple's GarageBand, you can try out your tempo with hundreds of prerecorded drum beats until you find one that matches the hymn. Of course, nothing informs the ear better than listening to pop radio, analyzing the grooves one hears.

There are as many interpretations of groove as there are musicians, but each hymn groove should demonstrate a thorough understanding of the original melody, using rhythms that complement and accent it. No more is needed or desirable for a tasteful arrangement. One would do well to follow the example of Robert Shaw and Alice Parker, whose choral arrangements of folk tunes met such tremendous success because of Shaw's insistence that the arrangement not draw attention to itself, but simply support the melody.

Change Chords

At the most rudimentary level, the hymn's existing harmonization can simply be reduced to chords that are more manageable by praise band guitarists. The hymn's original inverted, secondary, and substitute chords are all boiled down to their most basic elements—often the I, IV, and V chords—then transposed into a guitar-friendly key such as G, D, or E minor. This is the approach taken in *The Worship Team Hymnbook* produced by Christ Community Church in Franklin, Tennessee (available to download from www .communityworship.com), and many student-oriented songbooks. This is useful when only guitars are available to accompany singing but tend to neutralize all the unique characteristics of the original hymn. More satisfying chord choices can be made.

First, establish the hymn's harmonic rhythm, that is, the general rate at which the chords change. Typical four-voice hymn settings change chords with every note of the melody. In contrast, pop music (and therefore praise band settings of hymns) tends to change chords once or twice per measure. For example, "The King of Love My Shepherd Is" (St. Columba) can be effectively harmonized with one chord per measure:

1. The   King   of   love   my   Shep - herd   is,

Next, choose chords that fit the harmonic rhythm. Though the chords will generally change at the same rate throughout the song, there is certainly freedom to break the harmonic rhythm periodically. This is especially true of cadences, at which the harmonic rhythm is often doubled. Naturally, the primary goal is to choose chords that harmonize each note of the melody well. But the chords must also support the hymn's melodic structure. For example, "Come, Thou Fount of Every Blessing" (Nettleton) is in an AABA form, with a climax on the B section. Many harmonizations found in hymnals remain on the tonic (I) chord at the B section, but I prefer using the subdominant (IV) chord to highlight the change in form.

Finally, the new chords should support and interpret the mood of the original text and melody. Consider how different "The King of Love My Shepherd Is" (St. Columba) feels when the somewhat static harmonies found in most hymnals are replaced by the Celtic folk descending chord pattern shown above. Imagine how much less regal "Holy, Holy, Holy" (Nicaea) would sound if set to lush jazz harmonies. Because harmonic substance is directly related to emotional message, one should err on the side of restraint in order to let the text shine through.

Embellish

Once an appropriate groove and harmonies have been established, various embellishments can be considered. Introductions should prepare the tempo and spirit with which the congregation will sing. Short interludes (often called "turn-arounds" in jazz) between verses are sometimes appropriate, especially if the people will need a moment to catch their breath. Modulations can provide an exciting lift to the singing, provided they are not overused. Codas (also called tags) can be used to release the energy of the song, or even as a transition to another song. Descants and vocal harmonies (based on the new chords) can add further layers of musical interest just as they do in traditional hymnody.

There are a number of embellishments that individual musicians in the praise band will add intuitively. Chord voicings contribute a unique fingerprint to each new singing of the modified hymn, similar to the way the organ's voicing contributes its texture to the congregation's singing. Rhythmic ostinatos, called riffs in the pop world, can propel a hymn arrangement forward. Improvised melodic fragments, called fills, are regularly added ad hoc to a praise band's arrangement. If the new arrangement of the hymn is strong and clear, the individual musicians' contributions will only serve to strengthen the song, provided they don't overplay. Most important, their harmonies and improvisations must be based on the new chords.

As with any artistic endeavor, there is no right or wrong way to transplant a historic hymn into a contemporary praise band context. Perhaps it shouldn't be done at all in your worship context. If you do decide to lead hymns with the praise band, these principles will help you arrive at an aesthetically satisfying modernization that respects the original hymn and fits the praise band context.

7

REHEARSING AND LEADING

A professional baseball player doesn't just walk out on the field and play brilliantly; hours of exercise and training stand behind each split-second, game-changing play. In the same way, a worship team's potential effectiveness is determined long before its members enter the sanctuary on Sunday morning. With this in mind, in this chapter I'll concentrate more on the process leading up to a worship service than on worship leading itself.

Preparing for Rehearsal

There is a magic formula for leading effective rehearsals: thorough planning. Perhaps this is not the quick and easy formula for which you had hoped, but in a way it's good news. Worship leaders who don't have natural-born people skills or the ability to think well on their feet can still run effective rehearsals simply by preparing well. The race, after all, is not to the swift.

Over the years, I have developed a system of worship planning that has been very helpful. I begin with a year/season schedule sheet (long-term planning), which includes any major events—Christmas,

191

Sundays I'm away, or services that will be led by an outside group—
and themes or sermon series that will be explored in upcoming
months. Next I move my planning to a monthly planning sheet
(scheduling musicians and choosing music) that includes notes on
which musicians will be available for each service, brainstorms about
songs that could fit particular themes, and any nonmusical items that
will appear in the service such as stewardship reports. From those
rough drafts, I commit each week to its own sheet (finalizing the
service) that has details about the whole service, sometimes including
notes that will be helpful to me as I plan the rehearsal.

Long-Term Planning *(one to six months before service)*

Many worship leaders choose music a few hours before rehearsal.
I confess that I too have done this on occasion. However, long-term
planning is much more effective.

It allows more time for ideas to take shape. When you use a group
process in worship planning, all members of the planning team have
a chance to mull over service themes for a few weeks or months.
Even if you plan worship by yourself, you will find that ideas will
occur to you naturally—while you're driving or taking a shower for
instance—better than they do just hours before rehearsal.

It allows for more practice time. How often have you found the perfect
song for a particular worship service, only to realize that it is unfamiliar to your musicians and congregation? By planning worship a few
months in advance, you give yourself the lead time needed to teach the
song to your worship team and introduce it to the congregation.

It allows for "the big picture." Week-by-week planning usually
results in what Sally Morgenthaler calls "worship default." Worship default is what any church's worship will sink to when time,
creativity, and energy are not invested into the planning process.
You know how it works—you have an hour to choose music and
prepare for rehearsal, so you gravitate toward three or four of your
church's favorite praise songs and put them in the place that you
always sing them.

It allows more time for prayer. Many people give the impression
that planning worship months in advance is the domain of lifeless

religiosity. I would argue the opposite. The Holy Spirit can work as powerfully in worship planning as in a worship service. It is our job as worship planners to pray for the Spirit's guidance throughout the whole worship process.

Covenant Church in Pittsburgh is a good example of long-term planning. Many months before a new season begins they pray about the direction God is leading the church. Once a theme emerges, the church's artists begin to brainstorm about ways they could use the arts to highlight that theme. When the new theme is introduced, they release a CD featuring songs—many of them written by the church's musicians—that will be used in worship during the season. It is interesting to note that Covenant is a charismatic church; following the Spirit's leading can happen both within a worship service and before it!

Most of us don't have the resources to produce a CD every time the pastor begins a new sermon series. However, even the smallest churches have the ability to introduce a new song that will be used throughout a sermon series or liturgical season. And we can alert all the church's worship contributors—songwriters, banner makers, and poets—to themes for which they may have exciting materials to offer.

What do you do if your pastor's working style doesn't allow for long-range planning? One of the most common frustrations for music ministers is that they are hampered in their attempts at long-range planning because their pastors don't provide them service information in enough time to act on it. Some don't even know what the Scripture or theme of the service is until they hear it from the pulpit on Sunday morning. Frankly, this shows a lack of understanding—even a lack of respect—on the pastor's part. Pastors need to realize that it takes a long time to bring together the elements of a service. If that time is not available, the worship planner is forced to plan a "generic" worship service and hope for the best. It is simply in the best interest of the pastor to help the worship planner plan as far in advance as possible.

Unfortunately, there are no easy tricks to solving this situation. Some pastors prefer weekly meetings in which details of upcoming services are discussed. Others respond well to email requests. You may even need to use the church's secretary as a service planning "moderator."

Scheduling Musicians (one to three months before service)

While it is certainly possible to line up musicians the week of a rehearsal, it is much better to schedule them well in advance and plan music with them in mind. For example, if you know a month in advance that your regular drummer will be away on a particular Sunday, you'll have time to find—and perhaps train—a less experienced drummer. If you know your pianist will be gone, perhaps you could plan a service that features the acoustic guitar as the main chordal instrument. Long-range scheduling allows you to maximize your church's musicians and vary the sound of the ensemble slightly from week to week.

Choosing Music (two to four weeks before service)

A few weeks before a service, move from long-range brainstorming to fleshing out the details of the service. This is the "rough draft"—the point at which the service theme should be clearly articulated, the basic service shape established, and any pivotal music chosen. Say, for example, the theme of the service is "God's Word—a Foundation for Living." The service begins with a praise set that includes "Firm Foundation," the sermon is prepared by a soloist singing "Thy Word Is a Lamp Unto My Feet," and the service concludes with the congregation singing the first verse of "How Firm a Foundation," a cappella.

Finalizing the Service (week of service)

Put the finishing touches on your worship plans the week of the service. Flesh out any remaining music or worship elements and work to smooth the sections together for a service that flows well. Most important, check details of the service with the pastor and other staff members. It seems that every staff meeting brings surprise news about items that need to be included in the service, such as a special announcement or a word from a visiting missionary. Remain as flexible as possible. It is better to learn about these things during the week rather than a few moments before the service begins.

Preparing the Bulletin *(five to six days before service)*

Finally, the worship service is turned into a form that the congregation can use—the bulletin. You and the church secretary must work together to assemble a clear, error-free bulletin; it is the congregation's point of entry for worship. For example, when I began work at one church, I found out that for years they had been singing "You're my friend and You are my lover," rather than "friend and brother," in the song "As the Deer." Some of these problems can be avoided if you or the secretary keep master files of all the songs used in worship. As you discover mistakes, you can weed them from the master files. In the future, correct versions of the songs will be pasted into the bulletin. If your church uses PowerPoint rather than a bulletin, the same principles apply.

Preparing the Rehearsal *(day of rehearsal)*

Create a detailed rehearsal plan. Just as a teacher prepares a lesson plan that details the material to be covered and the methods used to teach it, worship team leaders should go into every rehearsal with a clear sense of what needs to be accomplished and how it will be accomplished. Typically the primary goal of the rehearsal will be perfecting music for the upcoming service, but there may be additional items such as learning new songs. A general rehearsal schedule should be established. The following is an example of what that might look like:

7:00 Prayer and discussion of previous service
7:15 Learn new song
7:45 Rhythm section works on transitions
         Vocalists learn harmonies in another room
8:15 Put it all together
8:50 Announcements and closing prayer

Each section of the rehearsal plan should include detailed notes of information that you need to communicate, specifics about transitions or instrumentation, or parts of songs you expect could cause problems. It might look something like this:

7:00 Prayer and discussion of previous service
 Remember to get an update on Joe's wife. Ask for other prayer concerns.
 Ask the vocalists if they were comfortable with the monitor mix this week.
 Bass—still too loud!

7:15 Learn new song
 Explain how I found the song, what it means, and how it fits into the theme.
 Read the Scripture it's based on.
 Point out the two places where the melody is tricky.
 Sing the song through quietly with piano.
 Go back to the tricky sections; do them slowly with, then without piano.
 Go back and sing entire melody when the musicians are ready.

7:45 Rhythm section works on groove and transitions
 New song: build groove from the bottom up. Don't move on until it's right!
 Point out that we have rushed "Song A" every time we've played it.
 Transitions: see rehearsal sheet. Make sure they write things down!
 Vocalists learn harmonies in another room (Joe's in charge). No harmonies on the new song!
 Polish harmonies on "Song A"—they've sounded out of tune the last few times.
 Try to memorize the new song.

8:15 Put it all together
 Talk them through the whole set.
 Remind them of the first transition and the a cappella ending.

Try running it.

Stand in the back and get a sense of the blend.

8:50 Announcements and closing prayer

Remind them that the sound check on Sunday starts at 8:15—not a minute later!

Read the email the pastor sent re how well the team has been doing.

Sing "Song X" as a benediction.

Assemble musicians' packets. At every rehearsal, each musician should have a packet waiting for them on their music stand. The packet should include all the material they need for the rehearsal: an annotated bulletin or set list, all music, and an upcoming schedule or newsletter.

The annotated bulletin and set list serve the same purpose of providing a road map for the upcoming service. The advantage of the annotated bulletin is that the musicians are reading from the same bulletin as the congregation. The only difference is that the worship team's version has copious notes about transitions, number of repeats, keys, and harmonies. Another advantage is that the musicians often catch misspellings and such before the bulletin is printed for the congregation. The chief disadvantage of the annotated bulletin is that the booklet format is difficult for the instrumentalists to juggle along with their music. It is easier for them to work with a set list. When printing a set list, use an oblong format that allows it to stick out a few inches beyond the music in their three-ring binder. All the song information—key, repeats, transitions—can still be seen as team members turn the pages of their music.

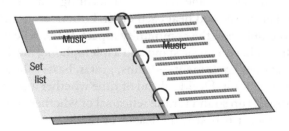

Include in the packet all the music the team will need for the rehearsal. Remember that each musician needs different formats of the music in their packet. The singers need words and melody, rhythm section needs leadsheets, guitarists may need transposed chords for playing with a capo, some pianists may need a piano arrangement, and additional instruments may need descants or transposed leadsheets. In order to save trees, you can encourage your musicians to keep a binder of all their music. Ideally, you will only need to copy new songs and a set list. However, my experience has been that only half the musicians will actually be willing or able to keep track of their own music and remember to bring it to rehearsal.

Finally, the rehearsal packet should include an upcoming schedule or newsletter. It may seem like a lot of work to write down every announcement you need to make, but some people simply respond better when they read something than when they hear it. I usually include information about upcoming services (Judy and John will be singing next week; there will be no rehearsal), prayer requests, and questions I want to remember to ask (Would all of you be interested in bringing your families to a picnic at my house next month? When would be the best time?). At times I've even produced a little newsletter that includes clippings from the newspaper about musicians' family members, or copies of kind notes that have been sent to me regarding the music ministry. People love to see their names in print, and reading about each other builds community.

Set up rehearsal area. It is important that your worship team arrives to a rehearsal space that is ready for music making. This creates an atmosphere immediately conducive to a productive rehearsal rather than the time-wasting chaos that ensues as volunteers try to figure out where they should stand and where equipment should go. Set up the rehearsal space ahead of time in a configuration that allows the musicians to see and hear each other. I often set up the team in a circle to emphasize the community aspect of the rehearsal. Each person should have a music stand and a microphone; musicians who bring their own equipment—drums, guitar, bass—should have a space set aside for it. Decide ahead of time whether a sound person will set up and run sound for the rehearsal or whether you will need to do that too. It is best if the leader of the team can concentrate fully on the rehearsal rather than taking up members' attention with sound issues.

Proofread Bulletin (after rehearsal)

Inevitably, rehearsal will uncover editing mistakes, lyric discrepancies, or worship changes. After the rehearsal, convey any of these bulletin changes to the church secretary.

Planning by Group Process

In many churches, one person—often called a music minister, worship leader, or director of worship—is in charge of all the tasks outlined in the previous sections. However, there is a growing trend for churches to plan worship by group process. There are many benefits to moving from the "Lone Ranger" approach to a collaborative model. A group process allows for a wider range of perspectives and areas of expertise and can lead to a stronger integration of the arts in worship. It also better represents the congregation and will foster a stronger sense of ownership in the worship "product" if the process is more inclusive.

A group process doesn't necessarily mean that a central music minister can't be involved. In fact, the process is often facilitated well by one person. For more information about making a collaborative worship-planning process work well in your church, see *Designing Worship Together* by Howard Vanderwell and Norma deWaal Malefyt (The Alban Institute, 2005).

Rehearsing

It is a daunting task to enter a room of mostly amateur musicians hoping to exit a few hours later with a polished set of music. Below are techniques that will facilitate the rehearsal process.

Organizing the Rehearsal Time

One of the keys to leading effective and enriching rehearsals is organizing the rehearsal time in a way that is conducive to achieving your rehearsal goals. Of course, you must first establish your rehearsal goals.

Practice? Prayer? Devotions? What is the right mix? Finding the right balance between spiritual and musical goals is a constant struggle for a worship leader. On the one hand, your team is under pressure to produce a high-quality praise set for the following Sunday—this is a significant musical challenge that requires ample rehearsal. On the other hand, the worship team is a spiritual entity, not a bar band. Ignoring the spiritual and communal aspect of the worship team betrays the fundamental nature of their work.

I find it helpful to think of this balance in terms of product and process. Yes, in the end, a "product" (a praise set) must be produced, but the process is more important because it shapes people. The process of coming together as a group and sharing your lives and struggles, submitting to one another in love, and joining together in diligent musical work will help the worship team musicians grow in their faith. When process takes precedence, the worship team will be healthy, and in the end they will bear the best fruit (product) they can give.

What does this mean in practical terms? That depends on the team and the leader. Many worship team musicians are involved in small groups, so it may not be necessary to have a full-blown Bible study—they are already getting that elsewhere. Instead, the worship leader can integrate the spiritual aspects of the worship team's work into rehearsal by discussing the meaning of a particular song text, taking time for prayer requests, and encouraging the team to communicate lovingly with one another. Another approach is to shape rehearsals themselves as a time of worship, with elements of invocation, prayer, Scripture, and benediction woven into the fabric of rehearsal.

However, some leaders feel very strongly that there should be a formal time of Bible study and prayer, perhaps even leading devotions on the topic of worship itself. This is certainly a good way to focus rehearsals on the right thing. No matter the final balance of elements, it is important that the worship leader encourages a rehearsal experience that is more than a musical rehearsal. Leading worship is more than music, so the spiritual components of worship leadership must be "practiced" as well.

Finding the best rehearsal structure. One of the most difficult aspects of worship team rehearsals is that the instrumentalists and vocalists need to rehearse vastly different things. While the instrumentalists need to work on grooves, transitions, and modulations, the vocalists need to learn words, melodies, and harmonies. Both can become frustrated and bored while waiting for the other to learn their parts. This boredom usually leads to talking and lack of focus that ultimately derails the whole rehearsal.

I have found three ways to deal with this problem. The first is to hold sectionals during the rehearsal time. For example, the worship team warms up together for a half hour, then the vocalists and instrumentalists work separately for an hour, and finally join for a half hour to put all the pieces together. Of course, this model necessitates a trusted co-leader; if there is no one on the team who can teach vocal harmonies or shape the band's groove, then it won't work.

An option similar to sectionals would be to simply hold two different rehearsals, one for vocalists and one for instrumentalists. There are some drawbacks to this approach, including the issues of team unity and putting the two groups together before leading worship. However, in a case in which split rehearsals were necessary because of scheduling conflicts, I found that it worked quite well. Our rehearsals were focused and productive, and the music came together easily during a pre-service warm-up.

A third option is to stagger the rehearsal. As shown in the graph below, the vocalists arrive later and stay later than the instrumentalists. This has the advantage of giving each section time to practice alone while also leaving significant time for group rehearsal. The disadvantage is that the rehearsals can feel disjointed with no precise starting and ending time. To combat this, I often have prayer and community time right when the vocalists arrive, and again when the instrumentalists leave.

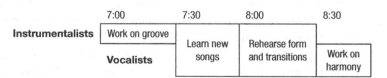

Leading Effective Rehearsals

Timothy Sharp, in his concise treatise on conducting, discusses the concept of "internalizing the score." After the conductor has studied the musical score, he creates the perfect performance of the piece in his mind. In this context, "a rehearsal becomes a comparison of the sound that is in one's mind (internalized sounds) to the sounds that are being made in the rehearsal setting (audible sounds)."[1]

The same is true of the worship team leader. He or she must be able to hear an ideal rendition of each song of the praise set before walking into rehearsal and then spend the rehearsal attempting to match that sound. To put it conversely, you won't get what you can't ask for. Of course, there will be many contributions from the worship team musicians during rehearsal, and the wise worship team leader will incorporate these ideas. However, beginning rehearsal without any idea of what you want is always disastrous.

Learn melody first. Many people think that jazz musicians just show up and jam, and somehow it all makes sense. In reality, each jazz musician knows the melody and chords of each tune inside and out; when they start improvising on a particular song, each musician has the tune ticking away in their head, providing a framework for their improvisation. In the same way, worship teams—both vocalists and instrumentalists—must learn the melody before working on other aspects of the arrangement. This gives the whole team a structure around which they can build their own parts.

Practice smart. If you want to learn an important lesson in musicianship, eavesdrop on a great musician's practice room. You will find that the best musicians rarely play through a whole piece in practice. Why? Because only small portions of the music give them trouble, so they concentrate their efforts on those portions. Many worship teams waste practice time *playing* rather than *practicing*. Rather than simply playing through songs from start to finish, the team should concentrate on the most difficult sections. For instance, setting a good tempo, transitioning, and modulating are all difficult—spend the bulk of the rehearsal on these things!

Learn songs once. I used to think that doing a song or praise set the same way twice indicated a lack of creativity. Then I learned a lesson from Bach. He recycled his own music regularly, changing the lyrics of an aria for use in a new setting, switching instruments for different ensembles, and extracting movements of old works for use in new ones. Now I approach each praise song arrangement or praise set as an "arrangement" that can and should be reused. For example, if your team has already worked out a groove and harmonies for a song, why spend the time relearning a new arrangement? If you used a three-song praise set on the majesty of God a few months earlier, why not use it again when it fits thematically?

This approach allows you to simply refresh the worship team's memory on old music, while concentrating more time polishing new music. Of course there will be times when you will want to create a brand-new arrangement for an old song, but, in general, you shouldn't try to reinvent the wheel every week.

Leading Enriching Rehearsals

Achieving week-to-week goals is certainly admirable, but what is the big picture of weekly rehearsal? If musicians are a part of your worship team for ten years, will there still be something valuable and enriching for them down the road?

Include time for non-Sunday rehearsal. The week-after-week grind of learning and perfecting music for the upcoming worship service can quickly become tiresome. As often as possible, leave time in rehearsal for things that are not of immediate use. For example, take a half hour to simply play through some new songs, and then ask the team for their opinion of the songs (and take their thoughts into consideration!). Set aside time for building general team skills in a fun way; for instance, use a song that everyone knows and try playing it in different styles—punk, country, salsa, and so on. Give the musicians an opportunity to build improvisation skills; play a four-measure chord sequence and let each musician have a chance to jam on it. I also find it helpful to have one "presentation" song that the team can work on over a few months. For example, have your team work on a Brooklyn Tabernacle Choir arrangement; the time spent honing a new style of music or working on a higher degree of polish will add to the musicians' experience and the team's skills.

Record your team periodically. There was a period in which one of my worship teams thought they were pretty hot stuff. All my rehearsal suggestions fell on deaf ears—after all, how could you improve on perfection? Then one night, I recorded the team's praise set at the end of rehearsal. As they listened, they realized that there was, perhaps, room for improvement. In fact, the musicians themselves began repeating all the things that I had been telling them for the last few months: "The vocals aren't blending." "The drums are too loud." "We play everything the same way." After that, they worked harder during rehearsals and trusted my suggestions more readily.

Recording your team quickly cures "good enough" attitudes, but it's also a way of letting each musician hear themselves—and the whole team—from a different perspective. It can be rewarding for the musicians to hear the results of their labors, and it often inspires them to reach for new levels of excellence.

Have fun (sometimes). I must admit, I'm a rehearsaholic. I very rarely cancel rehearsal, and I try my best to keep the team on task during rehearsal. However, sometimes a worship leader just needs to relax and get to know the team on a more personal level. This may mean taking the team out for ice cream, setting aside time in a rehearsal for an icebreaker, or spending time hanging out when rehearsal is through. These are the times that create community.

Be sensitive to your team's needs. Groups of people are just like individuals—they have moods and personalities. Be sensitive to the atmosphere at rehearsal, discerning if there are issues that need to be addressed. Sometimes the team needs to address conflicts that arise. Other times everybody is depressed or stressed out from work. The worship team leader is not a therapist, but he or she needs to be genuinely concerned about the welfare of the team and team members. If you sense team conflict or stress, stop rehearsal and ask them about it. If an individual seems down, talk to them privately. If a member misses rehearsal without alerting you, call them and make sure they're all right. This makes the difference between a music group and a ministry.

Leading Worship

I've been asked on numerous occasions what full-time music ministers do all week (by my wife, for instance . . .). The congregation sees us leading for an hour on Sunday morning—there can't possibly be thirty-nine hours of preparation for *that*! Hopefully, the preceding sections show that plenty of work takes place outside of Sunday morning. In fact, up-front worship leading is only the tip of the iceberg for a worship leader. Though much of what a worship leader does takes place outside of the public eye, there are certainly performance aspects of worship leading that require attention.

Preservice Warm-Up

A number of elements need to come together before the service starts.

Set up. The music equipment and sound system need to be set up and ready to go before the preservice warm-up begins. Each musician and the sound operator must know what tasks they are responsible for. Do instrumentalists only need to set up their own instruments? Do they need to be set up before the sound operator can set up? Are vocalists responsible for getting their own microphones and music stands?

The worship leader also needs to communicate with the rest of the church staff about anything else that needs to take place before the service. When do pastors and speakers check their microphones? Are there any other groups (drama, children's sermon, dance) that need to test sound or warm up before the service? When should the sanctuary be clear of rehearsals and be ready for worship?

Be on time. I've said this before, but the best way to encourage punctuality in your worship team is to model it yourself. It is especially important that everyone arrives on time for a preservice warm-up because time is always tight before church services. The later people arrive, the later the warm-up runs, creating a hectic atmosphere that isn't conducive to worship leading. Make sure you articulate frequently the time the warm-up begins, stressing that everything needs to be set up *before* that time.

Quickly rehearse beginnings, endings, and transitions. A worship team warm-up should remind the musicians of what was rehearsed previously. There is usually not enough time to play through the whole praise set. Instead, highlight the areas that you anticipate will cause difficulty. Make sure that tempos are correct and that introductions are secure. Remind each other of the form of each song. Work the transitions and modulations between songs, listening for solid entrances by the vocalists. Practice any tags or ritards at the ends of songs. One way to lead the warm-up effectively with a minimum of stops and discussion is to start the praise set at the beginning, calling out instructions as you go. For example, instead of repeating four verses and choruses as written, sing the first verse and then—without stopping the song—instruct the team to go directly to the fourth verse. This will cut rehearsal time in half, leaving time to touch up any spots that were rough.

Get a good sound check. Choirs and other acoustic ensembles can balance their sound by adjusting the dynamics within the ensemble, but worship teams are at the mercy of the sound system for achieving a balanced sound. It is imperative that they get a good sound check before leading worship. Ideally, the sound check begins during the weekly rehearsal where a sound operator is adjusting the sound and marking settings for Sunday's service, but having the same sound person for rehearsal and service is not always possible.

Many worship leaders and sound operators prefer to start the sound check by adjusting the monitors. The monitor system helps the musicians hear themselves and each other. Setting the monitor mix first allows the musicians to continue their warm-up while the sound operator moves on to the "house" mix (the speakers that point toward the congregation).

There are many different ways to mix the monitors, but in general the monitor mix will allow the vocalists to hear themselves and each other. It will boost any lead vocalists who may be giving important cues that the rest of the team needs to hear, and it will allow the whole ensemble to hear lead instruments like the piano or guitar. Musicians often need different monitor mixes. For example, the drums don't need to be amplified in the monitor, but the drummer needs to hear guitar and bass clearly in the monitor in order to stay in time. The pianist and acoustic guitarist may need some of themselves in the monitor, but the electric guitar and bass can monitor themselves from their own amps. The musicians should feel free to ask for adjustments in the monitor mix during the pre-service warm-up.

The worship leader can maximize the time spent on the sound check by using it as a rehearsal. For example, if the sound operator needs to work on the vocal blend, use it as an opportunity to rehearse a difficult harmony part. This gives the sound operator a chance to mix the sound based on something the vocalists will actually sing during the service and helps the vocalists warm up.

Potty, pause, and prayer. The time before a worship service can be hectic for the worship team, so they need a break before lead-ing. Fifteen minutes or so before the service starts, give your team a chance to go to the bathroom, relax, and collect their thoughts or chat. Shortly before the service, come together again for prayer.

Effective Song Leading

Common song-leading paradigms. Discussions of worship leader-ship often center on the musicianship or personality of the leader in question. These discussions should instead begin with the question, "What does the congregation need from the leader to sing well?" There are a number of approaches.

The *conductor* is a worship leader who leads the congregation like a choir, beating the tempo throughout each song. It often goes hand-in-hand with a congregation that sings hymns, usually sing-ing with great skill and enthusiasm. The advantage of this style of leading is that it gives clear musical leadership. The disadvantage is that it provides more information than the congregation needs and often focuses on musical leadership to the exclusion of other aspects of worship leadership.

The *cheerleader* is a worship leader, often associated with celebra-tory Praise & Worship or gospel songs, who pumps up the energy of the congregation with encouraging words and an upbeat demeanor. The advantage of this style is that the congregation often needs to be reminded of their role as active, enthusiastic worshipers. The disadvantage is that it focuses on eliciting a particular type of emotional response in worship. Can you imagine this type of worship leader cheering on other types of emotions? "Come on everyone, lament with your whole heart!"

The *entertainer* is a worship-leading paradigm that comes from the pop music world. In fact, many popular worship leaders today are "worship artists" or "worship personalities" who tour the country holding "concerts of praise" or "worship events." The advantage of this leadership style is that a winsome "lead worshiper" can encourage those in the pews to follow his or her example. The danger is that this strong up-front leadership—while exciting in a concert setting—may draw too much attention to the leader in a congregational worship context.

The *enlivener* is a worship-leading paradigm discussed in depth in Michael Hawn's *Gather into One*.[2] Most frequently seen in communal cultures in Africa and Latin America, the enlivener is not necessarily the best musician in the community but the person who most effectively draws everyone into participation. One sees an example of this in black gospel, where the worship leader's example is simply contagious. At its best, it draws people into worship without drawing attention to the worship leader.

These are common worship-leading paradigms. There is no absolute right or wrong style. In the end, each leader must find a comfortable leading style that gives the congregation what they need to participate in worship.

Though it is theoretically possible for a congregation to sing together without a leader, the Praise & Worship style usually requires up-front leadership of some sort. This doesn't mean that the worship leader should be the focus of the congregation's attention; it simply means that they know where to look if they need help.

The congregation usually only needs help starting or ending a song, or learning music that is unfamiliar. When starting a song, it is often helpful for the worship leader to raise his or her hand in a gesture of preparation and then cue the congregation to sing. On lesser entrances, the cue to enter can be given by simply looking at the congregation and breathing with them in preparation for singing. It is important that all the singers on the worship team begin each phrase confidently. I've attended worship services where the singers are so hesitant that the congregation doesn't enter until halfway through each line. If a song is new to the congregation or they are having problems with a line, the worship leader can lean into the mic and sing the melody more prominently to help them. Periodically, the worship leader will need to provide information about a song's form such as a repeat. This is especially true of churches whose worship is not mapped out in a bulletin or PowerPoint.

The worship leader's role is to help the congregation sing. If they're singing confidently, just back off from the mic and let them worship.

Increasing Team Communication

One of the greatest difficulties that worship teams face when leading worship is communicating with one another quickly.

Set up the team so they can see each other. The first step in tackling the communication issue is to arrange the members of the team in a way that is conducive to communication. The musicians should be fairly close to one another, as proximity is an important part of musical collaboration. The musicians should also be able to see each other or at the very least see the leader. Many teams set up in a semicircle with the leader in front. The problem with this is that the leader has to turn around to catch the team's eye. Some other possible configurations are arranging the whole group in a semicircle with the leader on one end, or a having a back semicircle of instrumentalists and a front row of singers. Experiment to find the setup that gives the leader a sight line to key musicians (piano and other vocalists, for instance) and gives the rest of the musicians proximity and sight lines to their closest collaborators (drums and bass, for example).

Appoint one leader. I'm always amazed when baseball players let a fly ball drop to the ground as they wait for the other person to catch it. The same kinds of errors happen in worship teams when no one is appointed to "call it." The team needs one person they can follow for tempos, cues, and quick decisions. Often it is the lead vocalist who can serve as a "conductor" for congregation and worship team simultaneously, but it could also be an instrumentalist in the back row who can communicate more effectively with the rest of the team. Leadership can even be distributed from week to week. The important thing is that the whole team knows where to look for cues or for help when things go awry.

Establish a repertoire of hand signals for quick, nonverbal communication. Each team member should know how to give and read a few hand gestures that communicate basic information such as "repeat," "instruments out," "faster," and "slower."[3] If the leader is playing an instrument, the gestures need to be adapted. For example, when I'm leading from the guitar my team knows that if I need to communicate something I will look at them and follow it with a quick gesture like tapping my foot in the tempo I want.

Insist on the team's full attention to each other. Stress to your team how important it is that they watch and listen to each other. Closing your eyes while you lead worship may seem spiritual, but it could leave you oblivious to the way the Spirit is moving in everyone else.

A good rule of thumb is that those who prepare well will lead well.

Once the service starts, no amount of worrying can make your leading more effective. Relax and enjoy the fruits of your labor. You have been blessed with the chance to worship God and facilitate others in their worship. What a privilege!

I'm a proponent of thorough preparation, but sometimes you simply need to change your plans. This is one of the exciting things about worship. God is a living God whose Holy Spirit moves in people. The congregation is a group of people with different personalities and moods. These dynamics can result in a very different atmosphere than you had planned. Instead of trying to force everyone to stick with your plan, follow them. This may mean repeating a song more times than you had anticipated, changing your funky arrangement of a song into a slow ballad, or even choosing a different song on the spot.

This gives all the more reason for your team to be attentive and have a repertoire of hand gestures for quick communication. It also suggests that it is wise to have at least a few songs memorized and rehearsed if needed for such occasions.

8

Looking to the Future

In the last forty years, Praise & Worship has gone from marginal to mainstream. Now there are new movements that arise from the margins. These movements won't replace Praise & Worship for some time, but they will exert increasing influence in coming years.

A New Generation of Worshipers

Though there has been an unprecedented rate of change in worship styles in recent years, it appears that even deeper and more significant changes are on the horizon. This is due in part to the massive cultural shift known as postmodernism.[1]

Postmodernism

Postmodernity stands in opposition to modernity, the age of reason and science that has ruled for the past two centuries. Whereas modernity values knowledge, postmodernity values experience. Modernity promotes individualism, postmodernity community. Observation versus participation. Text versus image. Logic versus story.

Worship leaders must be aware of this change in cultural climate, because it has a profound impact on the language we speak in worship. Leonard Sweet uses the acronym EPIC to describe postmodern worship: experiential, participatory, image-driven, and connected.[2] Though some lament certain aspects of postmodernism, in many ways it is good news for churches: the postmodern worshiper seeks an experience of God, participates wholeheartedly, and values the community of believers.

The Growth of Liturgical and Charismatic Worship

Previous generations came to church to learn, but postmoderns come to experience. They want to experience God in their senses— tasting the bread and wine, touching the cross, smelling candles burning. They want to feel God in their emotions. This desire for a worship experience that moves beyond the rational, involving the whole being, has generally led postmoderns in two directions: highly emotive worship styles such as those in Pentecostal or Charismatic churches or transcendent, mysterious experiences similar to those found in Orthodox or liturgical churches. Interestingly, both the Pentecostal and Orthodox have seen dramatic growth, whereas mainline denominations are shrinking at an alarming rate.

Increased Importance of Music

Music is taking more of a central role in today's worship. Today's worshipers are more likely to choose a church based on the quality and style of the music rather than the denomination or preaching. Fifty years ago this would have been unthinkable. Many churches have accommodated worshipers' musical preferences by creating different services that cater to specific tastes: contemporary, traditional, blended, and alternative.

However, this trend runs much deeper than musical preference. In a very real way, music mediates the worshiper's experience of God in the Praise & Worship context. The presence of God is almost invariably associated with music: "What a meaningful time of worship (i.e., musical worship) we had today"; "That worship leader really led me to the throne room"; "I could feel the Spirit's presence during that last song."

The new, elevated role that music plays means increased job security for worship leaders, but it is not without its problems. It may diminish the role (or the expectation) of other worship elements—most notably the preaching and sacraments. It can also become an emotional experience that has an almost addictive quality—one in which the worshiper returns again and again for a new "high" but never receives any spiritual sustenance.

Worship Industry

As music has grown more important to today's worshipers, the worship industry has grown as well. The worship industry has grown so powerful that it exerts extraordinary marketing pressure on local worship leaders: how can the worship leader resist a song that everyone in their congregation knows and loves from the radio? The industry has also become increasingly performer and performance oriented in recent years. This is not inherently bad, but it does place pressure on local churches to try to keep pace with the glitz of "worship artists."

Though the Praise & Worship genre dominates the charts and churches today, some question how long this can last. Like any popular music, it will gain momentum, become overplayed, then be replaced by a new fad—think Britney Spears, Garth Brooks, or the Partridge Family. As Mark Weber says so pointedly in a review of Matt Redman's CD *Where Angels Fear to Tread*, "In the music business—where money matters—Christian or not, it's time for a new trend. Praise & worship has lost its luster. Sorry. It has. It's all starting to sound the same."[3] Perhaps Weber's evaluation of the genre is overly negative, but there is an element of truth to his words. Any trend that so permeates its market will eventually become a caricature of itself rather than the refreshing expression it once was. My hope is that when the Praise & Worship style recedes, it will leave room for exciting and authentic local expressions of worship.

World Worship

We live in a global village. We can study in Japan, chat or video conference with someone in Australia, and buy goods from Iceland. As the distance between us shrinks, our musical interaction grows. This has exciting implications for Christian worship in America, as we are able to sing new songs that come to us from all over the world, including formerly "unreached peoples." Access to indigenous musics from around the globe has also expanded our range of instrumental possibilities. The sounds of the African djembe, Australian didgeri-doo, Mideastern chant, and Irish penny whistle have become common to our ears and are increasingly used in worship settings.

Convergence

Whereas previous generations experienced life and art in a linear fashion, people today are comfortable with a constant barrage of seem-ingly unrelated images, sounds, and words. For example, my seventy-year-old father found the few minutes of MTV he viewed confusing and disorienting. I, on the other hand, find that the combination of music, words, and images has an emotional impact that is lacking in his favorite movies and operas. People today are also used to the mixing of very different elements: Johnny Cash singing Nine Inch Nails or Moby creating techno pop from vintage blues recordings, for example.

The new generation of worshipers is open to any authentic musical expression: new, old, local, or foreign. Further, they are not concerned that all the music or worship elements are uniform in style. The most obvious manifestation of this is blended worship. However, this mix of music styles is just the beginning. High art and folk expressions can sit side by side in the service. Liturgical and Charismatic wor-ship can take place simultaneously. Any meaningful combination can be used and can deepen the worship experience.

The Next Generation of Worship Leaders

Just as the role of music in worship has changed dramatically and is continuing to evolve, the job description of the worship leader seems to be rewritten every day. A number of key issues will affect worship leaders in coming years.

Increased Importance of Worship Leaders

In days gone by the pastor chose the three hymns for the day, the choir director rehearsed the choir anthem, and the organist played a prelude and postlude. Little discussion was necessary. This "slot-filling" approach to worship has been replaced in most churches with worship planning that balances many different music styles, worship elements, and aesthetic sensibilities into one service—one in which a worship leader with musical skills and theological insight is needed.

More and more churches are realizing the advantages of having a worship specialist on staff rather than trying to plan worship with contributions from a number of volunteers. In fact, a worship leader or music minister is often the next position added after the pastor. In general, this is a healthy trend. Churches are making worship a priority and arranging their budgets accordingly. However, some churches view the worship position in an entirely utilitarian fashion: they value flashy programs that attract more people to the church rather than offering worship that pleases God.

The Worship Leader as Performer

Sometimes the importance of worship leaders turns into a "cult of personality" in which the worship leader becomes the center of attention rather than a facilitator for the congregation's worship. Perhaps this is a result of our passive, hero-obsessed society that would rather watch Michael Jordan play basketball than play basketball themselves. Regardless, there is something gravely wrong when people in the congregation "can't worship" because of the person leading or the style of music. This is a worship fetish—it is idolatry.

Granted, a worship leader should strive to have a good relationship with the congregation, developing a winsome stage presence. Above all, he or she should take care not to get in the way of the people's worship. Both the leader and the congregation should realize that the visible, up-front worship leadership is just the tip of the iceberg. Below the surface lies the bulk of the worship leader's ministry: praying, planning, and calling forth talents from the whole congregation.

Compensation, Respect, and Training for Worship Leaders

Ironically, though the importance of music and worship leaders continues to grow, many competent worship leaders work in less than professional situations. Pay lags far behind what is earned by workers inside or outside the church with comparable credentials. This may be changing somewhat in the church. It appears that churches are beginning to realize how important the arts are in worship, accepting the fact that improving the church's worship will require some financial commitment. Perhaps we will eventually return to a paradigm like that in the Baroque period; musicians and other artists were considered craftsmen and the church was their most significant patron. It is no wonder that this period produced musicians such as J. S. Bach!

Finally, we need to encourage—perhaps require—our worship leaders to receive adequate training. The number of colleges now offering worship majors is an encouraging sign that scores of worship leaders will be entering ministry with strong musical skills, biblical insight, and historical perspective. In decades past, worship leaders were primarily local musicians or music teachers who took part-time jobs in the church; they did an excellent job with choirs and instruments but often lacked pastoral skills or theological grounding. As the Praise & Worship genre has predominated in recent years, worship leaders were culled from the local rock music scene. These born-again band leaders have spiritual passion, but their musical skills are limited to pop and rock styles.

I don't believe it is too much to expect worship leaders to have training and experience in all the facets of a full-orbed music ministry. We should encourage musicians to be faithful with the gifts God has given them, and we should honor their efforts by paying them well for the work they do.

What's Next?

These are exciting—and sometimes unsettling—times for worship leaders. Christians have an awakened desire to worship in spirit and truth, yet there has never been more controversy over worship. There are new opportunities for worship leaders every day, but it is hardly a lucrative field. Worship is so simple, yet there are always a thousand new things to learn.

Be patient. Be faithful.

If God has called you into music ministry, he will lead you. He will bring you to the right church, and he will give you the strength and the wisdom to lead his people in worship. In the meantime, be faithful to the gifts God has given you. Study the Word, practice new musical skills, and learn everything you can about worship. Hopefully this book is part of that process, but it is only a starting point. Kevin Navarro identifies four areas of the "complete" worship leader: theology, discipleship, artistry, and leadership.[4] I think it is wise for every worship leader to invest energy into each of these areas, regardless of whether they've been doing it all their lives or have yet to set foot on their church's platform.

I pray that the next generation of worship leaders will be more faithful than my generation. That you will be as wise as serpents and as gentle as doves. That you will be stunning musicians, causing even unbelievers to ponder the source of your talent. That you will be humble servant leaders who build up the body of Christ. That you will write melodies of unsurpassed beauty and words that perspire with conviction. Above all, I pray that the triune God, who alone is worthy, will be praised on earth as in heaven.

Amen.

Notes

Introduction

1. The motto of the National Public Radio "Schickele Mix" program.
2. John Witvliet, "On Three Meanings of the Term Worship," *Reformed Worship* 56 (June 2000): 46–47.

Chapter 1 Setting the Stage

1. Charles Arn, "Selling Your New Idea," *Leadership Journal* (Spring 1999): 15.

Chapter 3 Building Repertoire

1. These categories are introduced in David W. Music and Milburn Price's *A Survey of Christian Hymnody* (Carol Stream, IL: Hope Publishing Company, 1999).
2. ©1990 Maranatha Praise, Inc. To review the lyrics, search for the title in Google.
3. "Why are you downcast, O my soul? Why so disturbed within me? Put your hope in God, for I will yet praise him, my Savior and my God" (NIV).
4. Ron Rienstra, "Remind Me—Why Are We Singing This Song?", Calvin Symposium on Worship and the Arts, January 13, 2001.
5. Cornelius Plantinga Jr., "Theological Particularities of Recent Hymnody," *The Hymn* 52, no. 4 (October 2001): 14–15.

6. Paul Westermeyer, *Open Questions in Worship: What Is "Contemporary" Worship?* (Minneapolis: Augsburg Fortress, 1995), 8–9.

7. Gary M. Burge, "Liturgical Worship: Using Ritual to Inspire True Worship," in *Experience God in Worship*, ed. Michael D. Warden (Loveland, CO: Group Publishing, Inc., 2000), 65.

8. Westermeyer, *Open Questions in Worship*, 11.

9. Thomas Day, *Why Catholics Can't Sing* (New York: Crossroad Publishing Co., 1992), 118–19.

10. John Bertalot, *John Bertalot's Immediately Practical Tips for Choral Directors* (Minneapolis: Augsburg Fortress, 1994), 60.

11. As quoted in Andrew Wilson-Dickson, *The Story of Christian Music* (Minneapolis: Fortress Press, 1996), 111.

12. As described in Jeff Todd Titon, ed., *Worlds of Music: An Introduction to the Music of the World's Peoples*, 3rd ed. (New York: Schirmer Books, 1996), 129ff. There is a recording of this extraordinary music on the CD that accompanies the book.

13. This relationship between harmony and rhythm can be seen clearly when observing the transformation of a lively, rhythmic, unison Lutheran tune such as Ein' Feste Burg ("A Mighty Fortress Is Our God") into the slow, solid four-part version of the hymn as we sing it today. It should be noted that some Lutherans are returning to the earlier version.

14. *Cow Joke Page!* 14 July 2002 <http://www.angelfire.com/music3/lfm/lfm_humor.htm>.

15. John Witvliet, "The Nuts and Bolts of Worship Planning," Calvin Symposium on Worship and the Arts, January 13, 2001.

16. Robert Webber, *Planning Blended Worship: The Creative Mixture of Old and New* (Nashville: Abingdon Press, 1998); John M. Frame, *Contemporary Worship Music: A Biblical Defense* (Phillipsburg, NJ: Presbyterian and Reformed Publishing, 1997).

17. One way to search for these church song lists is to type in two or three song titles, each title in quotes, in an Internet search engine. This returns both commercial and church sites that have these songs in their lists—they will also contain songs in similar style that may not be as familiar.

18. "Company History," <http://www.integritymusic.com/company/index.html>, 23 July 2002.

19. This slavery to the new is reflected in the advice given in "Hot Tips for Worship Leaders" (© 2000 Vineyard Music Group) where author Brent Helming recommends that one of the keys to great repertoire is a "mixture of both older (4 to 15 years) songs and newer (3 years to present)."

20. To order Taizé worship resources visit their website (http://www.taize.fr) or order through their U.S. publisher, GIA (http://www.giamusic.com).

21. Iona's music is published by the Wild Goose Resource Group and distributed by GIA (http://www.giamusic.com) in the United States.

22. Some excellent introductory collections of global worship music include *World Praise 2* (edited by David Peacock and Geoff Weaver, LifeWay, 2000), *Global*

Praise 1, 2, and *3* (edited by S. T. Kimbrough and Carlton Young, GBG Musik, 1996, 1997, and 2000) and *Halle, Halle: We Sing the World Round* (edited by C. Michael Hawn, Choristers Guild, 1999).

23. C. Michael Hawn, "A Survey of Trends in Recent Protestant Hymnals: International Hymnody," *The Hymn* 42, no. 4 (Oct. 1991): 24.

24. Malcolm Gladwell, *The Tipping Point: How Little Things Can Make a Big Difference* (Boston: Little, Brown and Company, 2000).

25. Marty Haugen, "Music from and for the World Church," National Association of Pastoral Musicians Omaha Regional Convention, July 9–12, 2002.

Chapter 4 Planning Worship

1. Webber, *Planning Blended Worship*, 79.

2. This is not to diminish the role of the Holy Spirit in other artistic creations; however, worship is an art form that *cannot* take place without the direct work of the Spirit.

3. In "The Worship Maze," Paul Basden lists five styles of worship: Liturgical, Traditional, Revivalist, Praise and Worship, and Seeker Service. Elmer Towns arrives at six paradigms of worship in "Putting an End to the Worship Wars": Evangelistic, Bible Expositional, Renewal, Body Life, Liturgical, and Congregational. Most similar to the categories discussed here, Barry Liesch identifies the Liturgical, Thematic, and Flowing Praise services on page 77 and following in "The New Worship." For an excellent discussion of various worship taxonomies, see "A Rose by Any Other Name: Attempts at Classifying North American Protestant Worship" by Lester Ruth, in *The Conviction of Things Not Seen: Worship and Ministry in the 21st Century*, ed. Todd E. Johnson (Grand Rapids: Brazos Press, 2002), 33–51.

4. Nicholas Wolterstorff, "The Reformed Liturgy," in *Major Themes in the Reformed Tradition*, ed. Donald K. McKim (Grand Rapids: Eerdmans, 1992), 275–76.

5. Doug and Tami Flather, *The Praise and Worship Team Instant Tune-Up* (Grand Rapids: Zondervan, 2002), 37.

6. John Witvliet, "At Play in the House of the Lord: Why Worship Matters," *Books and Culture* (Nov./Dec. 1998): 23.

7. See Michael S. Hamilton, "The Triumph of Praise Songs," *Christianity Today* (12 July 1999): 28; and Steve Rabey, "The Profits of Praise," *Christianity Today* (12 July 1999): 32.

8. See the following for further discussion of culture and worship: Marva J. Dawn, *Reaching Out without Dumbing Down: A Theology of Worship for the Turn-of-the-Century Culture* (Grand Rapids: Eerdmans, 1995); Calvin M. Johansson, *Discipling Music Ministry: Twenty-first Century Directions* (Peabody, MA: Hendrickson Publishers, Inc., 1992); Church Music National Conference (http://www.musiccrossroads.org).

9. Marilyn Chandler McEntyre, "Silence Is to Dwell In," *Christianity Today* (7 August 2000): 63.

Chapter 5 Making Music

1. Tom Kraeuter, *The Worship Leader's Handbook* (Lynnwood, WA: Emerald Books, 1997), 31.

2. Note that the technique for writing the Harmony Sandwich is identical to SAT Down, with the addition of a bass line doubling the soprano an octave below.

3. A pedal point is a type of dissonance that is commonly used by organ players (hence the name *pedal point*) in which one note—usually lower than the rest of the notes—is held while the chords above it change.

4. Advanced players can also play partial three- or four-string chords that rival the agility of the piano, but these players are rare. If melody, harmony, and specific chord inversions are needed—for instance, in a song introduction—it is usually safest to have a keyboard instrument play it rather than the guitar.

5. A plectrum, or "pick," is a thin piece of nylon a little bigger than a coin, held between the thumb and index and middle fingers.

6. For more information on using hand percussion in worship, see my article "Hands Around the World: An Introduction to African and Latin American Percussion in Worship" in *The Hymn* 57, no. 3 (Summer 2006).

7. Though the saxophone is technically a wind instrument, pop music traditionally includes it with the brass instruments.

8. Because mostly secular groups are setting the trends and perfecting the styles, it is probably more helpful to listen to them. I want to be cautious in recommending secular groups, because some of them are downright anti-Christian. However, if you believe that you are spiritually able to listen to the music without being negatively influenced, I would encourage you to do so. This is the best way to understand the modern music styles at a level this text can't provide.

Chapter 6 Timeless Hymns in a Contemporary Context

1. See Michael S. Hamilton, "The Triumph of Praise Songs," *Christianity Today* (12 July 1999): 28; and Steve Rabey, "The Profits of Praise," *Christianity Today* (12 July 1999): 32.

2. See Terry W. York, "Add One Hymn: Recipe for CCM and 'Modern Worship' Congregational Song," *The Hymn*, 55, no. 3 (July 2004): 29–33 and Gregory Rumburg, "All Things Bright and Beautiful: Today's Artists Dig into the Past to Make Sense of Today . . . and of the Future," *CCM Magazine* (March 2005): 26–33.

Chapter 7 Rehearsing and Leading

1. Timothy W. Sharp, *Precision Conducting: The Seven Disciplines of the Masterful Conductor* (Leawood, KS: Leawood Music Press, 1996), 22.

2. Michael C. Hawn, *Gather into One: Praying and Singing Globally* (Grand Rapids: Eerdmans, 2003), chapter 8, "The Church Musician as Enlivener."

3. These gestures are shown in *Songs for Praise and Worship, Worship Planner Edition* (Nashville: Word Music, 1992), 457–58.

Chapter 8 Looking to the Future

1. The postmodern ethos is often referred to as "emerging" or "emergent" when applied to worship.

2. Leonard Sweet, *Post-Modern Pilgrims: First Century Passion for the 21st Century Church* (Nashville: Broadman & Holman, 2000).

3. Mark Weber, "Redman's New CD Signals an End to the Praise & Worship Trend," 12 June 2003 <http://www.crosswalk.com/fun/1145916.html>.

4. Kevin J. Navarro, *The Complete Worship Leader* (Grand Rapids: Baker, 2001).

Greg Scheer (M.A., University of Pittsburgh) is a composer, church musician, and choir and music director who has served in several churches. He was director of music ministries and a professor at Northwestern College (Iowa) for five years. Scheer is currently minister of worship at Church of the Servant (CRC) and a music associate with the Calvin Institute of Christian Worship, both in Grand Rapids, Michigan.

A leader's guide for this book, including resources, reviews, and discussion questions is available at www.gregscheer.com